"This book will create a hunger for the Greater Glory and is also the 'go to' book to experience His Glory."

—Sid Roth, Host, *It's Supernatural!*

10 LEVELS

of

GLORY

DESTINY IMAGE BOOKS BY HRVOJE SIROVINA

Redeeming Your Bloodline

10 LEVELS

of

GLORY

CULTIVATING A LIFESTYLE OF
FACE-TO-FACE ENCOUNTERS
WITH GOD

HRVOJE SIROVINA

DESTINY IMAGE₀ PUBLISHERS, INC.
P.O. Box 310, Shippensburg, PA 17257-0310
"Promoting Inspired Lives."

This book and all other Destiny Image and Destiny Image Fiction books are available at Christian bookstores and distributors worldwide.

Cover design by Eileen Rockwell
Interior design by Susan Ramundo

For more information on foreign distributors, call 717-532-3040.
Reach us on the Internet: www.destinyimage.com.

ISBN 13 TP: 978-0-7684-5563-2
ISBN 13 eBook: 978-0-7684-5564-9
ISBN 13 HC: 978-0-7684-5566-3
ISBN 13 LP: 978-0-7684-5565-6

For Worldwide Distribution, Printed in the U.S.A.
1 2 3 4 5 6 7 8 / 25 24 23 22 21

CONTENTS

———◆———

Special Introduction *by Robert Henderson*   11

Introduction   17

What Is Glory?   23

More of the Glory   33

Level 1   Creation   57

Level 2   Signs and Wonders   65

Level 3   Experiencing God   79

Level 4   Knowing God   89

Level 5   Seeing God   107

Level 6   The Fear of the Lord   123

Level 7   Walking with God   143

Level 8   The Face of God   155

Level 9   Unity with God   171

Level 10   The Unapproachable Light   191

Paths to Greater Glory   197

Appendix   203

SPECIAL INTRODUCTION

by Robert Henderson

———◆———

When Moses requested of the Lord in Exodus 33:18 that He would "Show me your glory," this was a cry coming from the depths of his heart and spirit.

And he said, "Please, show me Your glory."

The Lord had agreed that He would send His presence with Moses and Israel. However, Moses desired the glory of God as well. This would mean that the presence of the Lord and the glory of God are different and separate realms that we can experience in the Lord. As God allowed His presence to be their companion, God said He would give them rest. This meant that the presence of God would keep them in peace, safety and security. This was a powerful promise. Still, however, Moses desired more. He wanted to experience the glory of God and what that entailed. The Lord agreed to the request of Moses and allowed Moses to see and encounter the glory. I believe that all people actually crave and desire to witness and partake of God's glory. This would especially be true of those who have been born again and have the new nature of the Lord living in them. One of the aspects of this nature is a groaning for the glory of God. We are told of this groaning and yearning in Second Corinthians 5:4-5. We are informed that those who belong to Jesus, even when things are at their best in this life, still long for a glory realm yet untouched.

> *For we who are in this tent groan, being burdened, not because we want to be unclothed, but further clothed, that mortality may be swallowed up by life. Now He who has prepared us for this very thing is God, who also has given us the Spirit as a guarantee.*

We are aspiring from the deepest places of our being, to be clothed again with the glory that was lost at the fall of man. Man was originally created to partake of the glory of God. Some would espouse that Adam and Eve were clothed with the glory of God and therefore required no natural clothings. When they sinned the glory was lost and their nakedness appeared. If this is true then this would mean man was made to live in and function from the glory of God. The longing Paul is alluding to is this restoration. This desire captures the heart of those who belong to God and causes them to seek that which we have yet to know. The Holy Spirit is given as a guarantee that God has made us and is preparing us for this glory. Holy Spirit is the firstfruits of that which we will ultimately live in and function from in times to come.

Some might be quick to point out that the Lord said, "He would not share His glory with another." This is found in Isaiah 42:6-8 where the Lord is speaking of His jealousy for His name and glory. This is actually a scripture speaking of the coming of Jesus as the Messiah.

I, the Lord, have called You in righteousness,

And will hold Your hand;

I will keep You and give You as a covenant to the people,

As a light to the Gentiles,

To open blind eyes,

To bring out prisoners from the prison,

Those who sit in darkness from the prison house.

I am the Lord, that is My name;

And My glory I will not give to another,

Nor My praise to carved images.

When Jesus came into the earth, He came to set prisoners free. He came to open blind eyes on every level. The Lord in a jealousy for His name refuses to allow idols and the demons they represent to claim the glory that is His. The Lord is jealous for His glory. This is why First Corinthians 1:27-29 tells us that God will not allow humans to boast and lay claim to that which His glory has produced.

But God has chosen the foolish things of the world to put to shame the wise, and God has chosen the weak things of the world to put to shame the things which are mighty; and the base things of the world and the things which are despised God has chosen, and the things which are not, to bring to nothing the things that are, that no flesh should glory in His presence.

The proud, arrogant and self-exalted ones have no rights in the glory of God. He will not share this with them. Only those who are humble, weak and even esteemed foolish does God trust with His glory. It would do us good to remember that Herod was severely punished when He refused to give glory to God that people were inappropriately heaping on him in Acts 12:21-23. As a result of him receiving the glory to himself, judgment fell upon him.

So on a set day Herod, arrayed in royal apparel, sat on his throne and gave an oration to them. And the people kept shouting, "The voice of a god and not of a man!" Then immediately an angel of the Lord struck him, because he did not give glory to God. And he was eaten by worms and died.

If we are to steward and partake of the glory of the Lord then we must do so in the fear of the Lord and with great sobriety. Kathryn Kuhlman is reported to have said that after her very powerful healing services, she would spend hours pouring the glory back out at the feet of Jesus. She understood she could not afford to receive any of it into her own spirit and being. If we are to partake of and steward the glory of God, it will require us walking in great humility and brokenness before the Lord. This is why we are warned in Philippians 2:3 of giving ourselves over to the pursuit of *vainglory.*

Let nothing be done through selfish ambition or conceit, but in lowliness of mind let each esteem others better than himself.

The words *selfish ambition* is the Greek word *kenodoxia.* It means "empty glory or vainglory." We are do do nothing to get the praise of men. This is empty and full of vanity. Our pursuit must be the praise of God which will result in partaking of His glory. John 12:42-43 shows us leaders in Jesus' day more concerned with the glory that came from men than the glory that came from God.

> *Nevertheless even among the rulers many believed in Him, but because of the Pharisees they did not confess Him, lest they should be put out of the synagogue; for they loved the praise of men more than the praise of God.*

This is the question we must ask ourselves. Do we desire the praise of men or the praise of God? Do we want the glory that men can give, which is fleeting, or the glory of God that is a stamp of His approval? In this book, Hrovje Sirovina depicts clearly the levels of glory that are available to us. The Bible clearly tells us in Second Corinthians 3:18 as New Testament believers that we are to go from glory to glory. This experience of His glory will continually change us into the very image of who He is.

> *But we all, with unveiled face, beholding as in a mirror the glory of the Lord, are being transformed into the same image from glory to glory, just as by the Spirit of the Lord.*

As we behold Him by the Spirit, there is a transforming that occurs. As we approach Him with an unveiled face, not afraid of our weakness, insufficiencies or places of rejections, the Holy Spirit will unveil Him and show us the glory of who He is progressively. We as with Moses will not just enjoy the rest of His presence, but also the power of His glory and majesty. Let us with Moses make our request that He might show us His glory.

Robert Henderson
Bestselling author, *Courts of Heaven* Series

INTRODUCTION

———◆———

Glory can be experienced. It moves us. It takes hold of us, and it changes us! What is this glory? It is when heaven and earth overlap and we witness the intervention of a supernatural, almighty, and eternal God in our natural and limited world.

My aim in writing this book is to familiarize us with this extraordinary and wonderful glory of God. Not for glory's sake, but for the Lord's sake. When we experience glory, it will inevitably generate hunger for more of Jesus. Glory is boundless, and this is why we should not be satisfied with the glory we are presently experiencing or enjoying, because in reality we are called to progress from glory to glory. On this journey to glory, the face of God becomes ever clearer to us, and at the same time we are being transformed—transformed into the image of Jesus. We are becoming more and more like Him.

On this journey to glory, the face of God becomes ever clearer to us, and at the same time we are being transformed— transformed into the image of Jesus.

I have experienced the glory of God in so many areas in such an amazing way, and yet it seems to me that I have only scratched the surface. That is how strongly the glory of God overflows! I have a deep desire for us, as the body of Christ, to experience more of it.

In Luke 5:17-26, Jesus healed a man who was paralyzed after forgiving his sins—something that amazed everyone who saw it but enraged the teachers of the law. Because only God can forgive sins, they believed Jesus was clearly guilty of blasphemy and deserved the death penalty. But by miraculously healing the paralyzed man, manifestly through the power of God, Jesus confused them. Obviously, unlike them, God took no offense at this—quite the contrary—He even affirmed Jesus by revealing His power through Him and healing the paralyzed man publicly.

And they were all amazed, and they glorified God and were filled with fear, saying, "We have seen strange things today!" (Luke 5:26)

They glorified God and were filled with fear, saying, "We have seen extraordinary things today." The Greek word used here for *extraordinary* is *paradoxos*; we are very familiar with its derivation, for example, in the word *paradoxical*. This word is a composition of *para* and *doxa*, in which *doxa* means "glory." Here they saw something paradoxical—something extraordinary, illogical, strange, a course of events contrary to their expectations. But it was the glory of God. Surely only God could forgive sins and do miracles like this. Therefore, Jesus was God. But how could God also be man? They were filled with awe.

This is often how we experience the glory of God. The German theologian Gerhard Kittel writes in his *Theological Dictionary of the New Testament*, "*paradoxos* is an unusual event that contradicts opinion and expectation; here it emphasizes how unprecedented Jesus' statement was."[1]

When we experience the glory of God, we cannot expect it to always make sense; quite often it can seem offensive to other people, even crazy, idiotic, or alienating.

But this is precisely the glory of Christ to which we are called—to extraordinary, unexpected, unusual, inexplicable, curious, strange, and sometimes contradictory and crazy moments and experiences with God (see 2 Thess. 2:14).

The fruit of this glory, however, is the fear of God and worship. They saw glory, something inexplicable; they glorified God and were filled with fear (see Luke 5:26).

The topic of "glory" is increasing in importance in the church, and several books about it exist already. However, I deliberately chose not to read anything about the glory of God so that I could write down almost exclusively what I personally sensed to be inspiration from the Holy Spirit through the written Word of God.

Two aspects are extremely important to me personally, and I hope I will be able to convey them in this book.

First, God does not withhold His glory from anyone. Everyone is predestined, called, and chosen to move from glory to glory, to experience God's miracles, and to be touched by Him personally. There are depths and levels of glory that seem to us to be too good to be true, and yet these very realms have been opened up to us by Christ. Chase after them, seek them, draw near to God, and you will be completely overwhelmed. If the church enters these realms to serve, rule, and bring change from there, the world will not be able to stand against the kingdom of God.

There are depths and levels of glory that seem to us to be too good to be true, and yet these very realms have been opened up to us by Christ.

Second, the glory of God is not cheap. Yes, God calls us from glory to glory, and He will not withhold it from us. Yes, thank God, there are certain realms of glory that we cannot escape; we are dependent on them, whether we are Christian or pagan.

But we should not make the mistake of selling the glory too cheaply or reducing it to goose bumps and feelings of happiness. It is still extremely sacred, precious, and of inestimable value. Do not be deceived—the highest areas of glory surely demand a price from us. A price that countless numbers of people have paid for Christ's sake. But it is worth it, because it fills us with life, true joy, unyielding faith, persevering trust, the meaning of life, inexhaustible love—and it drives away everything that stands in God's way. The glory of God opens up heaven on earth for you.

In this book I will try with earthly vocabulary to describe and reveal this heavenly allure of glory.

Language is a fascinating thing that enables us to communicate in many ways, to clarify ambiguities, and to define circumstances and facts in more detail. We use language to convey information, to speak prayers, and to make trite statements. Language is important and necessary, but at the same time not as logical as we would like to think it is.

We say, for example, that the nose runs and the feet smell, but it is exactly the other way around. Or is it? A juice made from oranges is what we call orange juice, but cough syrup is not made from coughs. The lapdog got its name because it sits on his owner's lap; however, the sled dog does not sit on the sled but pulls it. Have you ever noticed that before? I'll let everyone decide for themselves what they think.

You see, even language, as wonderful as it is, does not always seem as clear and understandable as we might expect. In addition, there is the discrepancy between what the speaker means and what the hearer "receives" or thinks he understands.

It's not all that simple.

And now I am going to try to describe something as exceptional as glory using this imperfect language, however wonderful it may be. Therefore, I put my trust in the Holy Spirit and ask the Lord to use this book to convey truths that go far beyond the written text.

I pray that God will use this book to speak personally to all the people who will hold it in their hands.

My prayer is that the Lord will fill people's hearts with truths about His glory.

I ask God to use this book, in spite of its imperfection, and to lead people into His glory, transform them, and kindle a fire in them so that they will not only plunder hell, but also set the world on fire and win it for Jesus.

NOTE

1. Gerhard Kittel, *Theologisches Wörterbuch zum Neuen Testament, Volume II*, s.v. παραδοξος (Stuttgart), 258.

WHAT IS GLORY?

—◆—

We already find it difficult to describe things or concepts such as beauty, games, or freedom; how much more complex it seems to me to try to adequately describe glory.

In order to explain beauty to someone who has never seen beauty before, we need to convey as much information as possible. The high mountains of Switzerland and the breathtaking nature of Austria with their wonderful colors, plants, forests, and fields without any doubt constitute beauty. And yet beauty cannot be limited exclusively to these beautiful colors and plants and certainly cannot be defined by them. The beaches of Thailand and the waters of the oceans are beautiful and yet have nothing in common with the expanse, mountains, and landscapes of Switzerland. We can associate beauty with people, things, feelings, smells, and much more, and yet it is not restricted to these; it is much more than all of them together.

We already find it difficult to describe beauty in its entirety and wholeness, and it is all the more difficult to find words for something that no one has yet seen or witnessed. How should we, as created beings with our limited means of expression, be able to communicate something as wonderful as the glory of God? Even C.S. Lewis said, "It's hard to look for something when you don't know what it looks like."

We can stand out rhetorically and poetically among billions of people and yet our words will not do justice to the glory. It is so wonderful, amazing, and perfect. Think about it—glory is so precious and holy and is worthy enough to surround the most outstanding being, God Himself, as it has done for eternity.

And although any formulations we may use will always remain inadequate, God will not withhold His glory from us. It even seems much easier to experience glory than to describe it. What is more, God has almost excluded the possibility of *not* experiencing it, because creation itself represents the glory of God and has been telling of it day in, day out for thousands of years. And yet it is impossible to grasp it.

The heavens declare the glory of God; and the firmament shows His handiwork (Psalm 19:1).

We can experience and even see the glory of God to a certain extent. It can touch us, change us, or completely blow us away so that our life will never be the same again. But it would be wrong to limit glory to certain personal experiences. Just as there is always more of God, and we will spend eternity experiencing and discovering even more of God, glory cannot be limited merely to individual experiences or events.

In the Old Testament, the Bible describes many moments in which people experienced extraordinary things with the glory of

God. We read in Second Chronicles 7 about the priests who could not perform their ministry because the glory of God filled the temple. The glory descended on the temple in a cloud of fire, which was visible to all Israel.

The prophet Ezekiel saw the glory of God, and in his prophetic book he described the experiences as well as the form of this glory (see Ezek. 1), but still today it ties our thoughts in knots when we try to imagine the wheel within the wheel and the eyes all around them.

The people of Israel were accompanied day and night by God's visible glory, which provided them with shade from the blazing sun and with warmth in the cold nights in the desert for 40 years. Another example is when Moses, Aaron, Nadab, and Abihu, accompanied by the 70 elders, climbed the mountain, saw God, and ate and drank with Him (see Exod. 24:9-11). What wonderful experiences, to name but a few.

Was all this the glory of God? Can we define that as "glory"? Of course it was—even God calls it glory, so there need not be two opinions about it. But even if this was all glory, there are even more glorious things, as Second Corinthians 3:9 makes clear to us.

For if the ministry of condemnation had glory, the ministry of righteousness exceeds much more in glory. For even what was made glorious had no glory in this respect, because of the glory that excels (2 Corinthians 3:9-10).

Was it the glory of God that the Israelites saw and testified about? Was the giving of the law at Sinai really the glory of God? Yes, and yes again. But in comparison to the Son of God, and in the light of Christ, it was a lesser glory. Jesus and the life in the New Covenant are so much more glorious than the law and what the prophets experienced that in the light of the eternal covenant, this glory loses so much radiance, not because it has become less glorious but because it has been unutterably surpassed in light and brilliance. Yes, it was the glory of God, but when you recognize the greater glory in Christ, it is difficult to call something that is of lesser radiance "glory."

Do not allow anything to stop you seeking for more of the glory of God. Do not be content with the level of glory you have experienced so far; however glorious it may seem, there is more. Go for it! Dare to ask for glory!

Do not be content with the level
of glory you have experienced so far;
however glorious it may seem, there is more.

DIFFERENT KINDS OF GLORY

I remember well when our son was born and we needed a larger car. A short time before that, we had experienced a financial breakthrough, which meant we could look for a nice car. Not much later we found the perfect car, which we were really happy about. It was not a luxury car from a prestigious German manufacturer, but still much better than our previous car. Our new car had plenty of space, very comfortable seats, and the rear seats were a real blessing even on longer journeys. A built-in GPS with a map setting function, parking sensors, and a hands-free telephone system were optional extras that we also enjoyed.

Even after three years we still felt totally blessed with the car, so that I even used to stand at the window of our apartment and look at the car and just feel grateful for such a great vehicle.

Until the last day we had it, it was such a great car, but after seven years it was time for a new one. My wife Ise had had a dream about a car in a certain color and with specific features, so we started looking for exactly this vehicle. This may sound a little naïve, but we believe that God often gives us impressions through dreams and, as it says in the Book of Job, dreams are God's way of speaking to us in the night (see Job 33:15-16).

After a few days we found exactly the car Ise had seen in her dream. It was such a great car, better than we could ever have imagined. The description of the extra features alone took up several pages. The electric leather seats were definitely a step up from the comfortable seats of our old car, and not only that, they also had a memory function that immediately recognized whether Ise or I got into the car, so that the seats were automatically adjusted to the respective driver.

For unlocking and starting the car we no longer had to use the key—you only needed to have it in your pocket. The lane-keeping assist system helped us to keep to the lane boundary when driving, and if you did drift a little too far to the right or left, the car recognized this, and with smooth but certain pressure, the steering corrected the position. An electric tailgate and a panorama roof were just a few more features we enjoyed.

For several days we owned two cars, because it took us some time to sell our old car. Our old car was a huge blessing right to the end, and we had never felt that it was an old or bad car. But when we got used to the comfort and the equipment of the new car and had enjoyed that for a while, our point of view instinctively changed. I can still remember exactly how it felt after only driving the new car for a few days and then sitting in the old car again. It was as if my eyes had been opened. Out of the blue, the old car seemed really old. The comfortable seats were suddenly no longer as comfortable, the ride left much to be desired, to say the least. From one day to the next I noticed sounds like squeaking, creaking, and grating—and I hadn't even been aware of them until then.

What had changed? Had our old car worn out faster in a few days than it had done in the years before? No, of course not. It was my perception and the comparison I was using. What I had considered to be comfortable, I no longer felt was comfortable. The pleasure with which I had driven the car had gone, and it wasn't the car's fault. The new car was to blame. It had opened a whole new dimension to me, and what had previously been luxury suddenly was no longer so. In the light of the glory of the new car, the old one was no longer glorious.

That's what glory is like. Second Corinthians 3:18 says:

But we all, with unveiled face, beholding as in a mirror the glory of the Lord, are being transformed into the same image from glory to glory, just as by the Spirit of the Lord.

It is not God's desire to show us glory just so that we know what it is. Rather, He wants to encourage us to strive for glory and to experience glory. Then, when we discover it, God wants us to keep going and develop a greater desire to search for more. When we make progress, the splendor of the new glory suddenly makes the old seem less glorious.

That is why it is so difficult to find a definition or description for glory that does justice to it. With each attempt, I would feel I was limiting and restricting His glory, because it is so much more than words put together to define it. I would totally fail if I maintained that I could describe glory.

But if I had to try, then my attempt would look something like this: Glory is love, grace, mercy, righteousness, justice, riches, holiness, selflessness, renown, honor, worship, reverence, majesty, power, strength, salvation, redemption, forgiveness, provision, peace, overcoming, victory, light, life, joy, contentment, warmth, confidence, fulfillment, and then so much more, all united in a single thing that we then call glory. Glory is when heaven overlaps with earth and we experience something extraordinary—God's supernatural intervention in our simple and natural world.

Glory is when heaven overlaps
with earth and we experience something
extraordinary—God's supernatural intervention
in our simple and natural world.

I once heard someone say, "What blue is to the sky, light to the sun, wetness to water, that is glory to God. Without God there is no glory, and yet God is much more than glory." I don't know how much sense this statement makes, but somehow I like it and it makes me dream of God's incredible greatness.

But what I do know is this: Glory in its completeness and physical or natural form is a person—the man Jesus Christ. Without Jesus there is no glory, and if we want more of His glory then we need more of Him.

Glory can be experienced and is comprehensible; in this book I would like to describe ten levels of the glory of God that He has enabled me to identify in the Word of God.

I pray that God will open our eyes and make us aware of His glory, which is already all around us, before our eyes, and which we have overlooked day in, day out. But my request goes even further—I pray that the glory of God will fill the earth and take hold of people to an extent that we have never seen before.

If you want to progress from glory to glory and learn more about the glory of God, I invite you to read on, but be careful.

Glory is not always as cheap as we would like it to be, but believe me, it is worth paying the price!

MORE OF THE GLORY

———◆———

And he said, "Please, show me Your glory" (Exodus 33:18).

Charles Haddon Spurgeon, an English Baptist pastor and perhaps the most famous preacher of the 19th century, said this was the greatest prayer a person has ever prayed.

It is not for me to judge whether Spurgeon's opinion is right or wrong or whether Jesus' prayers were greater or not. But it shows me that Spurgeon knew something about the glory of God that moved him to make this statement. Had he had a personal encounter with the glory of God, or had intensive Bible study led him to his conviction? I don't know, but Moses' prayer was surely one of the most inspired and innovative requests a person ever made to God. But when we look at the choice of words, the request of Moses seems to be less a request and more a heartfelt plea.

Why was Moses' request so amazing? At first sight, the words do not seem very weighty, as in many Christian circles today there is much and frequent talk about glory. But in Moses' case it is not the words that we read—it is the whole background to his pleading that makes it so amazing.

Only seven verses before this famous event we read about God's relationship with Moses.

So the Lord spoke to Moses face to face, as a man speaks to his friend (Exodus 33:11).

Here is a man, a friend of God, who knows God to be on his side and is speaking face to face with the Creator of heaven and earth, with the most glorious, almighty, and perfect being from whom nothing is hidden and who cannot be surprised by anything, because He is omniscient and our hearts are like an open book before Him. He looked into the eyes of God, he hung on every word of the Almighty, he absorbed the goodness and holiness of the Perfect One, and he was moved by the righteousness of the Creator of all things.

In spite of all these experiences, in spite of this amazing relationship, and in spite of these desirable experiences, an unquenchable desire had developed in the heart of Moses—he wanted more!

Isn't it already glorious to speak with God face to face? Oh, there's no question about it—of course it is! Isn't it glory when we are allowed to see God and to communicate with Him? No question— yes, it is! All the miracles Moses was allowed to witness—aren't they all the glory of God? There cannot be any other understanding of this: Yes, that is the glory of God!

But how, after all these experiences, could Moses beg God to please show him His glory? Was all that not enough already? That's the point. No, it wasn't enough for him! He was not content with what he knew, what he had experienced, and what he could testify to. He did not harden his heart before God, and thus every experience only produced more hunger, thirst, and desire. No matter how glorious the glory that he experienced, Moses did not want to stop there. He wanted more because God still has more! He was not satisfied with the past and present encounters. He wanted to penetrate still deeper into God, even at the risk that it might cost him his life.

WALKING IN GOD'S WAYS

Verses 11 to 18 of Exodus 33 reveal so much about Moses. In verse 11, we catch a glimpse of Moses' wonderful relationship with God. Verse 18 gives us insights into Moses' hunger and unquenchable longing to see more of God. But it is probably the statement we read in verse 13 that is most impressive, for it reveals Moses' heart and attitude.

Now therefore, I pray, if I have found grace in Your sight, show me now Your way (Exodus 33:13).

Before Moses asked for more glory, he wanted to know God's ways. This is what is really fascinating. Experiencing the greatness and glory of God and seeing God face to face did not awaken any selfish motives, desires, inclinations, or longing in Moses. It created selflessness. He didn't want his own will; he wanted God's will. He wasn't looking for his own ways; he was looking for God's ways. He wasn't interested in his own wishes, but God's wishes. He subordinated his plans and opinions to the plans of God.

This is the attitude that will make you thirsty for more of God and that enables us to strive for any level of glory at all, for which it is worth giving up everything and for which so many heroes of faith were willing to sacrifice their lives.

Now the man Moses was very humble, more than all men who were on the face of the earth (Numbers 12:3).

What a statement about Moses! He could have simply enjoyed a luxurious life in the house of Pharaoh, not having to give a thought to the people of Israel as long as everything went well for him. Instead, he did not let the fire inside him die. At the beginning, he did not know how to deal with it, and out of human sympathy he lost his composure and killed an Egyptian overseer. Forty years later he was in exile, but now God had someone He could use, because Moses had caught fire and was moved—he allowed himself to be moved.

GLORY IS MEASURABLE

When people experience the glory of God in such a deep way, it will not go unnoticed. I am convinced that it is possible to assess how much glory people have experienced. It is measurable by means of our character; in Moses it was measurable—he was the humblest man in the whole world.

But we all, with unveiled face, beholding as in a mirror the glory of the Lord, are being transformed into the same image from glory to glory, just as by the Spirit of the Lord (2 Corinthians 3:18).

When you look at glory, you are automatically transformed, you no longer remain the same—and you no longer want to be the same. The more glory, the more we will become like our King Jesus.

The measure of glory that we have experienced and seen is shown by whether we love more and resent less, forgive more and condemn less, are more generous and act less selfishly, develop more trust and are guided less by fear, and accept more and accuse less. How much glory we have experienced is measured by our character and whether it has become more like Jesus.

With the glory of God, your life and your faith will change. Jesus is no longer your religion; He will become your friend. We will no longer use God as our stooge; He will become our Lord. Our relationship to Jesus will no longer be through an icon or a saintly image, but through the Word of God as He becomes our example. Jesus is then no longer just a part, but really everything in our lives.

Jesus is no longer your religion;
He will become your friend.

THE OMNIPRESENCE OF GOD

There is no place where God is not. The psalmist wrote so aptly in Psalm 139:

Where can I go from Your Spirit?
Or where can I flee from Your presence?
If I ascend into heaven, You are there;
If I make my bed in hell, behold, You are there.
If I take the wings of the morning,
And dwell in the uttermost parts of the sea,
Even there Your hand shall lead me,
And Your right hand shall hold me (Psalm 139:7-10).

David had the advantage that he had already known God and worshiped God passionately. He tried to grasp the greatness and sublimeness of God by writing wonderful poetry about God, life, and God's relationship to people and nature.

But even if people do not experience and recognize God's presence, and even deny it, He is still omnipresent. In fact, the presence of God is essential for our lives, and woe betide us if God withdrew Himself and withdrew His presence from us, for there would be no life, no light, no radiance. Indeed, there wouldn't even be drought, desert, or wasteland. There would just be nothing.

For by Him all things were created that are in heaven and that are on earth, visible and invisible, whether thrones or dominions or principalities or powers. All things were created through Him and for Him. And He is before all things, and in Him all things consist (Colossians 1:16-17).

No life without God. No creation without God. Without God—simply nothing.

The "omnipresence of God" does not necessarily involve an awareness of God or an experience with God, nor does it imply a recognition of truth.

In the omnipresence of God, we can even live a life completely without God. We can disavow Him, doubt Him, completely deny Him, and, yes, even curse Him, as so many do. It is possible to be totally convinced of God's non-existence, even though He is omnipresent, in every place at the same time, whether in the past, present, or future. He has always been, is always, and will always be in the time to come.

It is God's love and grace that permits us human beings to live even if we do not care about God or human beings and if we are evil or even a blot on the world. God graces us with His omnipresence, because without it nothing is possible.

THE EXPERIENTIAL PRESENCE OF GOD

Then there is a presence of God that I call the "experiential presence of God." I am convinced that no one can escape this presence either. It is found in these moments when supernatural things happen.

> *But Jesus' answer to them was this, "My Father is still at work and therefore I work as well"* (John 5:17 PNT).

God is constantly at work and so is Jesus. There are no moments when God is on vacation, withdraws, or takes a break. It is God's nature to work, and it is impossible for Him to stop, whether we are aware of it or not.

In my view, the Book of Esther best reflects this aspect of God's presence. In this whole book you are looking for God to intervene, and it seems that God is not doing any obvious miracle, because no specific miracle is recorded there.

And what is even more amazing is that throughout the book there is no mention of prayer, praise, repentance, sacrifice, or worship, and to make it even more extraordinary, God is not mentioned in a single verse in this book. It seems as if God is not present, or at least not consciously present. You look for God in the Book of Esther and He seems nonexistent.

But just here is the mystery—even if God does not seem to be present, He is still omnipresent. Although He did not work an obvious miracle, God miraculously saved His people.

God directed events like a brilliant director; He put the scenes and circumstances together as if there was no way of escape for His people, but everything God did was brilliantly planned, just as a director is not visible in the film, but you know that his hand was in every scene. He knows the script and he has decided the end before the beginning.

That's often the way it is with God. He is the most important person on the set, and a film cannot be made without His guidance; in His mind He knows exactly what the scenes should be like. The director is the most important person in the movie, but he is not seen once in the movie. Even when the tension and uncertainty for everyone else increases, the director knows exactly how it will end. And in exactly this way, God had planned the salvation of the Jews at the time of Esther. Not only did He plan it, the Jews also experienced it!

Many, or even most people experience God in one way or another without ever becoming aware of it or meeting God personally.

They do not recognize God in these experiences. But because it is definitely an amazing experience for them, alternative terms are often assigned to this intervention by God. Instead of attributing it to God, people call these events coincidence or luck. Other expressions are "incredible," "at the right time in the right place," "guardian angel" (which often describes what really happened), "supernatural," "aura," or "it just happened," etc. Almost all religions were founded on the basis of supernatural experiences. Individuals experienced something supernatural, which was often God's tangible presence, but even in God's experiential presence they did not recognize the truth.

> *So that they should seek the Lord, in the hope that they might grope for Him and find Him, though He is not far from each one of us* (Acts 17:27).

God is not far from us; He is actually very close to us—and even more than that, we are constantly surrounded by Him. We have the possibility and the ability to take one more step beyond these realms of the presence and to recognize truth; this truth then becomes apparent at the next level of the presence of God. This is the personal presence of God.

PERSONAL PRESENCE OF GOD

Although God has been omnipresent since eternity and we cannot even escape His presence, there have nonetheless always been places where God has chosen to reveal His personal and more intense presence.

Below is a passage that I wrote for my wife's book *Haus, Gemeinde, Ekklesia* [House, Church, Ecclesia]. It describes this personal presence of God:

We know that omnipresence is one of God's characteristics, which means that He is here, in the present and everywhere in one and the same period of time. With this presence He keeps humanity, the earth, and the universe alive and functioning. And yet there is this one special expression of the presence of God, which is more tangible, more experiential, more intense, and more special than His omnipresence. It is the atmosphere in which one feels as if time is standing still. It is this realm in which you are quiet and encounter God in a personal way.

At the time of Moses, God was just as omnipresent as before, and this state has not changed until today. And yet, there have always been these special places where, in the omnipresence of God, one could break through into a more intense presence and experience a personal encounter. Israel was in the omnipresence of God, but there was a personal presence in the tabernacle. This was the place of the special presence of God and of encounter with Him. The garden of Eden was this realm for Adam and Eve; Enoch also found this place in his life; for Jacob, it was Bethel; for the Israelites, the tabernacle; for the chief priests, the holy of holies, and for David, the tabernacle of David, to name but a few.

That's exactly what God is looking for today. He wants to give us joy through presence, in which people can have an incredible encounter with Him. A presence that completely transforms us, in which we receive hope, receive faith, draw strength, attain vision, but are also healed, cleansed, and sanctified.

And suddenly a light shone around him from heaven. Then he fell to the ground, and heard a voice saying to him, "Saul, Saul, why are you persecuting Me?" And he said, "Who are You, Lord?" Then the Lord said, "I am Jesus, whom you are persecuting" (Acts 9:3-5).

God wants to give us joy through presence, in which people can have an incredible encounter with Him.

Not everyone has such a testimony of the personal presence of God as Saul. Suddenly Saul was startled by God's personal presence. He did not just feel or merely imagine this encounter; it was literally an appearance of Jesus, whom Saul saw with his physical eyes and his companions perceived acoustically with their ears.

My own encounter with the personal presence of God was certainly not as dramatic, but it shook me no less to the foundations of my lifestyle. I grew up in a Roman Catholic family—praying, going to church, rosaries, as well as crosses were part of the permanent inventory of our lives. I was definitely a believer and I was not ashamed of it—frankly, I was even proud of it and didn't understand at all how someone could *not* believe.

Eternal life and heaven had always fascinated me, but I was quite afraid of hell. I encouraged friends who were in difficulties to pray the Lord's Prayer, because for God no difficulty is too great. I was aware of God's presence and did not doubt God's intervention through His perceptible presence—and yet I did not know God's personal presence until the nineteenth year of my life.

Faith was important to me, Jesus was my hero, and I did not doubt God. And yet my life did not reflect my faith. From year to year I began to do more and more things that did not honor God and even displeased Him. Stealing, lying, visiting the red-light district, and other things increasingly became part of my lifestyle, and I didn't really even feel bad about them. Until this one Friday—March 16, 2001—that was the day I was born again and first encountered the personal presence of God.

Until the evening my day had gone as usual, and nothing indicated that it would be the most important day in my life. I had arranged to meet my friends in the evening to party in a club, and before that we would hang out for fun in a strip club before we turned night to day. The weekend was always the highlight of our week and we could hardly wait for it.

My sister invited me to a meeting on that day, March 16. In the weeks before that, I had already noticed how much she was changing. Her grumpy expression had given way to laughter, contentment, and happiness. Instead of hanging out with unsavory friends outside, she preferred to read the Bible and go to prayer meetings and spent her free time praying and talking about Jesus instead of zapping around pointlessly on the TV.

After being asked several times to come to a meeting like this, I gave in and promised her I would be there on March 16 but would not spend the whole evening there. So that I would not get bored, I took eight or nine friends with me, who all accompanied me to this church meeting.

Before the meeting started, we sat down in the last row of chairs, intending to leave a short time afterward to have a blast later that night. My mother was sitting in one of the middle rows of chairs, and when I saw her I went over to tell her something. But when I wanted to return to sit with my buddies, the meeting suddenly started and somehow it seemed inappropriate to go back to my original seat, so I remained seated beside my mother.

And then it happened: In the midst of the omnipresence and experiential presence of God, the personal presence of God filled the room, and not only that—it touched me, it took hold of me, it captured me. God took hold of me and He didn't intend to let go of me again. I have no idea what the preacher was talking about, but from the moment the event started, I had a lump in my throat that only went away when I let the tears run freely.

God, whom I believed in and whose existence I did not doubt, suddenly became real to me; He surprised me by meeting me in His personal presence. I was neither searching for the meaning of life nor was I in a depressive phase. I would not have wanted my childhood to be any different; I was popular, had friends and family with whom I felt secure, I was not faced with a hopeless life situation, and I was enjoying life. I wasn't crying out to God because of a crisis, nor was I looking for a way out. God had simply decided it was my time.

Of course, I had experienced disappointments, and I didn't feel completely fulfilled during all the nights of partying, but there were no overwhelming feelings that I was having to deal with daily. I noticed this vacuum only in quiet moments, and apart from that I did not pay any attention to it. There was also no special music or atmosphere in the room that might have touched my feelings. The sovereign God simply decided to reveal Himself to me through His personal presence in this building—in a room where I had been so many times before, because it was owned by the Croatian Catholic Mission and used as a parish building.

There really was nothing about this "basement room" that might suggest an encounter with God. And yet it was there that this Almighty God laid His finger on my heart and asked me to open my heart for Him. Everything else is simply gratitude.

My friends left the meeting in the course of the evening, but I stayed and also attended the meetings on the following days. There were some who had similar experiences to me on those days, but most people left as they had come.

Why was that? Why were some overpowered and taken hold of by God, and at the same time others noticed nothing? I don't know the answer to the question "Why?" I only know that there is a difference between the omnipresence, the experiential presence, and the personal presence of God, and God visited some of us with His personal presence in the midst of His omnipresence, while for some it did not go beyond that.

Since then, everyone around could testify that something momentous happened in my life. Some people liked it, many did not, and others could not deal with it at all. I would never presume to equate myself with the men and women of God who did great things, but somehow the above-mentioned reactions to such events seem to follow regularly—we read this in the Acts of the Apostles and we find it in church history. Some perceive it with joy; others develop a deep aversion to it.

So this was my encounter with the personal presence of God. These days were like an earthquake for me, and basically that's what it was. Not everyone has such cataclysmic encounters with God. For some it is merely a decision without much fuss, but it is no less a profound decision. Whatever it looks and feels like, when people welcome Jesus into their hearts in the personal presence of God and are born anew, all heaven becomes a party mile.

Likewise, I say to you, there is joy in the presence of the angels of God over one sinner who repents (Luke 15:10).

THE SCARING PRESENCE OF GOD

God seems to have made it quite easy for people to experience His presence, to be saved, and to develop a personal relationship with Him—all of this is remarkably uncomplicated, because it is God who positively invites us to do so.

However, there is another presence there that God almost dissuades us from, even making it unattractive for the most part. I call it "the scaring or hidden presence of God."

Please do not misunderstand me as saying God wants to withhold this presence from us—not at all. He only wants to protect us, which is why God hides this form of His presence from us and does not make it easy for us to enter it.

Clouds and darkness surround Him; righteousness and justice are the foundation of His throne (Psalm 97:2).

Then it came to pass on the third day, in the morning, that there were thunderings and lightnings, and a thick cloud on the mountain; and the sound of the trumpet was very loud, so that all the people who were in the camp trembled. And Moses brought the people out of the camp to meet with God, and they stood at the foot of the mountain (Exodus 19:16-17).

This presence is surrounded by clouds and darkness, by lightning and thunder, by the sound of loud trumpets and noise.

God is so incredibly holy that it is impossible for something to exist in His presence that is not itself equally holy. He is so unbelievably righteous; something that does not correspond to His righteousness cannot exist before Him. The Lord is so wonderful that it is unimaginable that we humans—imperfect beings that we are—could survive in this presence. It is precisely for this reason that He reveals to us step by step different characteristics of His presence in order to lead us gradually even further into it.

The Lord is so wonderful that it is unimaginable that we humans—imperfect beings that we are—could survive in this presence.

When we begin to understand what an incomprehensible God the Lord is, we know why it is necessary to progress from glory to glory and why we cannot simply jump into the highest measure of glory. As we move from glory to glory, we are gradually and slowly transformed so that we can be led into the next dimension of glory.

The personal presence of God is vital for us to be able to recognize the Almighty God as Father and provider; there we learn to be accepted and loved and to lay aside rejection. But in the scaring presence, it is no longer about us; here it is about Him and Him alone. Without doubt, the personal presence of God changes us, but the scaring presence of God transforms us from our innermost parts to the last fiber of our being. Nothing remains as it once was.

When Israel camped at Mount Sinai, they had already experienced the presence of God in the form of signs and miracles, and also the personal presence of God when they confessed Him as their only God, who had personally protected them from all the plagues in Egypt and afterward provided for them in the desert. But God wanted to take them one step further; He intended to lead them into His scaring or hidden presence. For this to happen, they had to be willing to be a people of priests, a holy nation:

"'You have seen what I did to the Egyptians, and how I bore you on eagles' wings and brought you to Myself. Now therefore, if you will indeed obey My voice and keep My covenant, then you shall be a special treasure to Me above all people; for all the earth is Mine. And you shall be to Me a kingdom of priests and a holy nation.' These are the words which you shall speak to the children of Israel." So Moses came and called for the elders of

the people, and laid before them all these words which the Lord commanded him. Then all the people answered together and said, "All that the Lord has spoken we will do." So Moses brought back the words of the people to the Lord (Exodus 19:4-8).

Their experiences with God were immense; they witnessed daily the supernatural overlapping the natural. In view of these experiences, who would refuse God's request for a nation of priests? Of course, all Israel agreed with God's desire.

For three days they purified and sanctified themselves in order to finally appear before God, as He intended.

Everything was prepared for this meeting, and God wanted to lead His people to the next level of glory, a glory that is hidden in the fearsome presence. Israel stood there, and God came closer and closer to them.

Now all the people witnessed the thunderings, the lightning flashes, the sound of the trumpet, and the mountain smoking; and when the people saw it, they trembled and stood afar off. Then they said to Moses, "You speak with us, and we will hear; but let not God speak with us, lest we die." And Moses said to the people, "Do not fear; for God has come to test you, and that His fear may be before you, so that you may not sin." So the people stood afar off, but Moses drew near the thick darkness where God was (Exodus 20:18-21).

What the people saw, and what this presence sparked off in them, frightened them away. There was no secretion of happiness hormones (endorphins) and no goose bumps, no gold dust or angel feathers, and also no voices of an angel choir; there was fear and trembling that shook them to the core. They saw themselves in the light of the glory and holiness of God and began to be afraid.

There is a presence and form of the glory of God that we cannot deal with lightly. God must scare us so that we tremble with awe. This presence is not just for everyone who believes in God or has experienced the personal presence of God. Neither is it for those who find Jesus cool and even love Him in some way. This presence is for people who fear God and whose lifestyle is holiness and sanctification because their God is holy.

The holiness of this presence is also clearly illustrated by the story of Ananias and Saphira in Acts 5. Things that are apparently not avenged in the omnipresence, the experiential presence, or even in the personal presence have immediate consequences in the scaring presence. This presence is so holy that God must deter us from it so that we do not approach it carelessly.

I once heard about a pastor who was in prison for embezzlement of funds. After some time, a pastor, who was a friend, visited him and wanted to know how he had come to commit this crime. He asked his friend when he had stopped loving Jesus. The pastor replied in surprise: "Never, I have never stopped loving Jesus," and added, "but I stopped *fearing* Him!"

There are areas of the glory of God that are so wonderful that we cannot endure them through love alone—we need the fear of the Lord.

This is a presence that does not come cheap. We cannot escape the omnipresence and experiential presence of God; this is God's grace, and not only since the time of Noah—it is God's eternal covenant with the world, which He maintains in every moment of world history, regardless of whether humankind perceives and respects it.

This is a presence that does not come cheap.

By contrast, access to God's personal presence was made quite easy for us, although it was still not cheap. It cost the Son of Man His life. It was by no means cheap; it required the highest possible price—the life of Jesus on the cross. The scaring or hidden presence of God cost Jesus His life, and if we want to experience it in the same way then it requires from us a price that is no less great. Not that we would all have to die a martyr's death, but this presence is exclusively for those who submit their life to God alone and make it available only to Him. Everything in their life belongs to God, and they withhold nothing from Him.

This has nothing to do with salvation; in salvation there is no work that we can add, it is exclusively God's work. Salvation is the prerequisite for this hidden presence, but it does cost us something.

It is an incredibly high price that not many will be willing to pay, but these are the very people who will set the ball rolling so as to shake the world to its foundations. In this presence there are the last four dimensions or levels of the glory of God that I will describe in the coming chapters. Not everyone will be willing to pursue them, but for those who choose to do so, their reward and place in heaven will be of immeasurable value and renown. Perhaps the earth will disregard their value, disparage them, or even denigrate them, but heaven, eternity, even God Himself will prepare a place for them, a robe, a victor's wreath, and renown, for which all others will wish they had given their lives as well.

This presence and these realms of glory are not reserved only for a chosen elite but are for everyone who is willing to give up everything else for it.

Are you ready? Is that the kind of person you want to be? Then get ready and take hold of it and dare to ask for glory!

CREATION

And one cried to another and said: "Holy, holy, holy is the Lord of hosts; The whole earth is full of His glory!" (Isaiah 6:3)

This is a celestial scene taking place among the seraphim. They are calling out, "Holy, holy, holy is the Lord of hosts." They are rejoicing, singing, and cheering, but they are not rejoicing and raising their voices to the Lord. It says that they were calling out to each other. They call out to each other as if they were stunned by the glory of the Lord, as if they could not stop marveling. We are not told why they are calling out to one another. We can only surmise or guess the reason.

Maybe they're looking out for each other to be holy themselves because God is holy. Perhaps they are calling to each other so as never to deviate from what the meaning of life is—to glorify God and to be available to Him. We don't know and maybe the idea I have described doesn't correspond to your theological understanding of angelic beings—that could be—I have simply expressed my thoughts here without a filter. The sight of seraphim calling out, "Holy, holy, holy is the Lord of hosts" to one another both fascinates and amazes me.

Seraphim and cherubim are angelic beings who are closer to the throne of God than most others are permitted to be. They have the privilege of witnessing firsthand the works of God.

> ***Where were you when I laid the foundations of the earth?*** *Tell Me, if you have understanding. Who determined its measurements? Surely you know! Or who stretched the line upon it? To what were its foundations fastened?* ***Or who laid its cornerstone, when the morning stars sang together, and all the sons of God shouted for joy?*** (Job 38:4-7)

They "sat" in the front row and experienced live and firsthand God creating the earth. Because they see God, are in His presence, and can tell of His actions, they look to the earth and can tell us that the whole earth is filled with the glory of God. Creation, the visible world, is a form of the glory of God, not like that on Mount Sinai at the time of Moses or the glory of the heavenly Jerusalem and Mount Zion, but it is glory.

Both natural wealth and physical riches are called glory in the Bible.

> *Do not be afraid when one becomes rich, when the glory of his house is increased; for when he dies he shall carry nothing away; his glory shall not descend after him* (Psalm 49:16-17).

It may be a lower form of glory that is left behind when we enter eternity, but it is glory. At the same time, however, we must not lose sight of the fact that the most valuable natural things are often those that are of least value in heaven.

The twelve gates were twelve pearls: each individual gate was of one pearl. And the street of the city was pure gold, like transparent glass (Revelation 21:21).

What is more brilliant on earth than gold and gems? Some of them are invaluable. But in heaven they are merely the building material for roads and walls. John the Baptist was the greatest man born by a woman, but in the kingdom of heaven, which surpasses natural creation, he was the least significant. The most valuable thing on earth is the least valuable thing in heaven.

Assuredly, I say to you, among those born of women there has not risen one greater than John the Baptist; but he who is least in the kingdom of heaven is greater than he (Matthew 11:11).

**What is more brilliant on earth than gold and gems?
But in heaven they are merely the building
material for roads and walls.**

Yes, creation is glory, but in its lowest form and appearance. We also see how God attributes glory to other parts of His creation, such as persons (see Dan. 2:37), kingdoms (see Ps. 145:11), children (see

Hos. 9:11), or nations (see Isa. 17:4). How could it be otherwise? When God creates something, then it must carry glory and bear witness to it.

For since the creation of the world His invisible attributes are clearly seen, being understood by the things that are made, even His eternal power and Godhead, so that they are without excuse (Romans 1:20).

DO NOT BE BLINDED

But precisely because God's creation is so wonderful and glorious, there is often the danger of getting absorbed by or lost in its beauty and thus missing God's power and divinity. Many scientists are completely mistaken and deny God's creative influence on nature. They are totally overpowered by the complexity and phenomena of created things and are blinded by that. Perhaps I am too simple in my thinking to leave God out of creation. That may be, and I am not a scientist either, but it is hard for me to be satisfied with denying a supernatural Creator simply because we can explain natural phenomena.

I like the way Dr. John Lennox, a professor of mathematics at Oxford University and a Christian apologist, explains it. Lennox believes that the attempt to explain God away because the processes of His creation can be proved scientifically is comparable to the attempt to deny Picasso's existence because the composition of the colors of his paintings can be explained scientifically. If creation is God's painting and we understand some of its procedures, it is naïve to deduce the absence of this supernatural artist. It is impossible to infer the absence of an artist from his works of art, even if, as in the case of Picasso and many other painters, he is no longer visible.

I love the creation account in the Bible. It is not a complete and detailed account of how God created everything and put into practice, and it is impossible to deduce from it all the wonders that God has created, but with the creation account He gives us so much capacity to marvel and meditate. The purpose of the creation account is not that God is explaining to us scientifically how the beginnings of creation can be explained—probably not even all the books in the world would be adequate for this complexity.

But what we do learn is, there is a Creator behind all of this. The whole natural world is not based on chance but on an inconceivably perfect and ingenious being.

For by Him all things were created that are in heaven and that are on earth, visible and invisible, whether thrones or dominions or principalities or powers. All things were created through Him and for Him. And He is before all things, and in Him all things consist (Colossians 1:16-17).

And this being is a person—the Father, the Son, and the Holy Spirit.

HIDDEN IN THE VISIBLE

But even if the account of creation is quite brief. Taking up just a little more than one chapter, God conveys some important messages and mysteries to us in it.

God begins by forming the heavens and the earth out of Himself. On the first day, He created the light and separated it from the darkness. On the second day, God made the sky in the form of a vault that separated the waters below and above the vault. On the third, God collected the water in one place, so that the land emerged. Also on the third day, God created grass, herbs, seeds, trees, and fruit, all of which sprouted out of the earth.

Then God said, "Let the earth bring forth grass, the herb that yields seed, and the fruit tree that yields fruit according to its kind, whose seed is in itself, on the earth"; and it was so. And the earth brought forth grass, the herb that yields seed according to its kind, and the tree that yields fruit, whose seed is in itself according to its kind. And God saw that it was good. So the evening and the morning were the third day (Genesis 1:11-13).

From a scientific point of view, we would already have to intervene here and explain to God that He had done things in the wrong order. This is, of course, only meant hypothetically, as we know that God does not make mistakes; instead, there is a revelation in the creation order.

If we look at days three and four of creation, then God would have had to create the sun, the moon, and the stars on the third day before continuing with the creation of grasses, trees, and herbs. We already learn at school that in order for grasses, trees, herbs, and seeds to sprout, they need energy from light, preferably sunlight. However, this did not yet exist on the third day, although it is absolutely necessary for the biochemical process of photosynthesis for the production and building of energy-rich organic compounds from low-energy inorganic substances.

Energy-rich organic substances are vital and life-sustaining components of plants. This sounds quite complex for non-scientists, and it is complex; nevertheless, I will describe it here briefly, even at the risk of depicting it too primitively. Without the sun there is no photosynthesis and therefore no life—and without life there is no growth. Period.

So God should have created the sun, the moon, and the stars before He created the plants, because they are vital for the sustenance and growth of the plants.

Behind the glory of creation
there is an even greater glory that is invisible
but cannot be limited by what is visible.

But God does it exactly the other way around to show us that behind the glory of creation there is an even greater glory that is invisible but cannot be limited by what is visible. It is the glory of light from the first day of creation, a glory that is more dynamic than the light of suns, moons, and stars. The 60th chapter of the Book of Isaiah describes the effects of future glory.

The sun shall no longer be your light by day, nor for brightness shall the moon give light to you; but the Lord will be to you an everlasting light, and your God your glory. Your sun shall no longer go down, nor shall your moon withdraw itself; for the Lord will be your everlasting light (Isaiah 60:19-20).

What God is saying is, there is a transcendent glory that cannot be grasped scientifically or is perhaps not yet tangible. But it is more life-giving and more glorious than what can be explained in the natural. We often call the effects of this life-giving light "supernatural" or "a mystery." Which brings us to our second level of glory—signs and wonders.

LEVEL 2

SIGNS AND WONDERS

It may be surprising for many people to see signs and wonders described as the second level of God's glory and not being categorized at a higher level.

But before I go into this in more detail, we want to identify signs and wonders as part of the glory of God. To do so, we will read about the beginning of Jesus' earthly ministry in the gospel of John.

After Jesus had called the first disciples, they followed Him a few days later to a wedding at Cana in Galilee. At the celebration, those present enjoyed the delicious food, the abundant drinks, the music, the dancing, and the fellowship with the other guests. It seems there was a pleasant atmosphere in which the wedding party consumed more of the available wine than the groom had planned for in advance. Of course, this is a most unpleasant situation for the host, and to rescue him from this embarrassment Jesus used the opportunity to perform a previously unseen miracle with which He began His ministry on earth.

Jesus said to them, "Fill the waterpots with water." And they filled them up to the brim. And He said to them, "Draw some out now, and take it to the master of the feast." And they took it. When the master of the feast had tasted the water that was made wine, and did not know where it came from (but the servants who had drawn the water knew), the master of the feast called the bridegroom. … This beginning of signs Jesus did in Cana of Galilee, and manifested His glory; and His disciples believed in Him (John 2:7-9, 11).

Jesus revealed His glory in the form of a sign and a miracle. In this form of glory, the heavenly and the earthly realms overlap. The invisible heaven intervenes in visible nature and breaks through natural limitations; for a short time, it suspends its laws without completely abrogating them.

The benefits of this glory seem to be limited almost exclusively to earthly and temporal matters. Of course, diseases and physical limitations may prevent us from spreading the kingdom of God (which would very well be of eternal value), but physical healing, opening blind eyes and deaf ears, the multiplication of food, raising the dead, casting out demons, walking on water, and turning water into wine—all these seem in most cases to be limited to earthly things.

Even if the benefits seem restricted to life in the here and now, these miracles still pursue the goal of leading us to the next levels of glory, a more glorious and precious glory, namely to faith and salvation, and these undoubtedly are of eternal and immeasurable value.

Then Jesus said to him, "Unless you people see signs and wonders, you will by no means believe" (John 4:48).

Yes, when He does miracles, God is proclaiming, "I am far superior to the devil." And by this, the demonic powers also lose parts of their territory and we can take these for God's kingdom. But what use is it to us if we are freed from physical suffering throughout our lives but do not attain eternal salvation (or lose it)? What will the pleasure and wellbeing of 80 years of this life bring us if we miss the glory of the eternal kingdom?

What use is it to us if we are freed from physical suffering throughout our lives but do not attain eternal salvation?

MIRACLES ARE THE GLORY OF GOD

Please don't get me wrong. I believe in signs and wonders. We should seek them and resist the lies of the devil, who wants to hold back miracles from us and persuade us that they are no longer for this era. Healing is precious, worth striving for, and available to people, for Jesus was whipped so that we might be healed by His stripes (see 1 Pet. 2:24). That alone makes me an advocate of signs and wonders. I want Jesus to receive the reward for all the sufferings He endured for us. He traded His justice for our guilt, His life for our death, His wealth for our poverty, His blessing for our curse, His well-being for our pain, and His health for our diseases.

In the last almost two decades I have witnessed incredible miracles: people who regained their sight, who were cured of tumors and cancer, who experienced supernatural material or financial increase, who got out of wheelchairs and started to walk again after years. I saw shortened legs growing out, headaches disappear in an instant, migraine attacks never returning, damaged teeth restored, slipped discs regressed, and dead people coming back to life. I saw how hopeless situations were remedied, people were covered in gold dust, angelic choirs sang, angels appeared, heavenly scents could be smelled, and on a cloudless day during a sermon thunder sounded, to name but a few.

All this strengthened my faith and trust in God, although these had never been dependent on signs and wonders. I never doubted God's sovereignty, even if many things did not make sense to me.

And yet there are many who doubt or wonder about the meaning of God's supernatural intervention. It is criticized, and people point to the danger of seeking signs and miracles instead of God.

This is a legitimate objection, but at the same time we could apply this to all other areas of our Christian life. Many people are so fixated on the Word of God that it lost all its power and finally mutated to nothing more than dead theology. Others made prayer such a strong tradition that they lost their personal relationship with God. Some, on the other hand, are so eager to accomplish the works of Jesus that they lose their souls. Then there are those who chase exclusively after spiritual things so that they ultimately lose any earthly value for their fellow human beings.

Should we stop reading the Word of God just because there are people who twist its meaning? Or should we stop praying, doing the works of Jesus, and seeking the heavenly things just because it dragged many people out of a balanced lifestyle? Of course not! And neither should we stop believing in signs and miracles just because there are some who have made it their primary focus in life.

Even with Jesus we could often ask about the point of His signs and miracles, which we of course will not do, but I mention it here purely for the sake of completeness. In John 12:37, for example, a great multitude of people did not believe despite the countless miracles that Jesus performed. But if there was only one person who began to believe, then we should not question the purpose of signs and miracles, because that should be more than enough.

And as already mentioned above, this benefit really appears to be almost exclusively of earthly use, but it has the power to open the hearts of men to truth and faith. If God gives us signs and miracles merely to demonstrate to us His care, grace, mercy, and love, and nothing more, then this should be reason enough for us to seek signs and miracles.

*If God gives us signs and miracles
merely to demonstrate to us His care, grace,
mercy, and love, and nothing more,
then this should be reason enough for us
to seek signs and miracles.*

MIRACLES ARE NOT EVERYTHING

Yes, it is my conviction that faith and discipleship are more important than signs and miracles. Faith is greater glory than signs and wonders, but Jesus used them in the past and He still does so to bring people to the next level of glory. This again does not mean that we exclude signs and miracles or completely ignore them. How could we, when they are also a secondary effect of our faith?

And these signs will follow those who believe: In My name they will cast out demons; they will speak with new tongues; they will take up serpents; and if they drink anything deadly, it will by no means hurt them; they will lay hands on the sick, and they will recover (Mark 16:17-18).

Signs and miracles of all kinds should be an integral part of Christian life. If we are followers of Jesus, then we should inevitably have personal testimonies about God's miraculous love and power in our lives.

Jesus' character is reflected in passion for God and in love and compassion for people. It shouldn't leave us cold when we see people in trouble or suffering. Jesus came with solutions, and countless times He came with the glory of signs and wonders, healing every sickness and every infirmity (see Matt. 9:35). He was involved in people's lives, took time for their needs, and did not turn away any sick person who came to Him or was brought to him, but He healed them all (see Matt. 14:14; 12:15; 8:16).

Do you believe in Jesus and are you a follower of Jesus? Then the second level of the glory of God is open to you. Perhaps you are one of the few who can reveal this glory to the people around you—then summon up your courage, ask God for Jesus' love and passion for people, trust God, and become the channel through whom signs and wonders flow into the world.

You have a name at your disposal that God has exalted above all names, and every knee, whether in heaven or on earth or below the earth, must bow to that name—before the name of Jesus (see Phil. 2:9-10). In this name you cast out demons, in this name you speak in new languages, in this name you lay hands on the weak and they will recover. This glory is at your disposal.

There are areas of God's glory for which we must pay a high price if we want to experience them. The highest levels of the glory of God are undoubtedly not cheap and sometimes require immense personal sacrifices; but signs, miracles, and healings—for these, Jesus has already paid the price.

MIRACLES ARE FOR EVERYONE

Salvation is the prerequisite for eternal life, and faith and our confession are needed for salvation. The bar doesn't seem to be really high in this case. It seems even easier with signs, miracles, and healings. Yes, we often read how people actively came to Jesus, which was an act of faith for receiving their miracle, and Jesus rewarded them for their efforts.

All too often, Jesus seems to urge people to allow Him to do a miracle. In John 5 we read of a man who had been afflicted with an illness for 38 years. The text does not tell us what kind of illness it was; we can only assume that it made him extremely weak and limited his everyday life. Like many others, he came regularly to the pool of Bethesda in the hope of receiving his miracle through the "healing water." Anyone who got into the pool immediately after the water had been seen to be moving could be sure of being healed. But this is a man who never made it into the water among all the sick, blind, lame, and weak people. This fact shows us how much he was suffering.

And then Jesus appeared. From the appearance of the needy man He recognized how long the illness had already been afflicting him. Jesus asked him if he wanted to get well, which is an interesting question, because the people who gathered at this place were mainly those who in their despair were looking for nothing else. Apparently unaware of who was standing before him, the sick man replied with an excuse as to why the miracle did not work for him. And as if Jesus had not paid any attention to the answer, He commanded him to get up, to take his bed, and walk. The man was instantly healed.

What amazes me about this story is that the man did not look for Jesus; Jesus came to him. He did not know or recognize Jesus, but Jesus was interested in him. Doubts and excuses instead of faith had already found their way into the thoughts and language of the needy man, but Jesus overlooked them and healed him anyway. The text also suggests to us that his gratitude was limited, for when asked about his healing he did not even know to whom he owed it. Jesus still cared for him nonetheless.

We would say that this sick person did not fulfil a single condition for receiving his miracle. That's true! And Jesus healed him anyway. Healing is for God's whole creation and not only for God's children. Signs and miracles are not limited exclusively to very, very holy servants of God. Healing is for the whole world, and the world only needs you and me who bear the name of Jesus and in this name courageously bring the healing of God to people.

Healing is for God's whole creation
and not only for God's children.

73

HEALED FOR SALVATION

The following story from Luke 17:11-19 confirms this. There, Jesus meets ten lepers who are in great need.

Now it happened as He went to Jerusalem that He passed through the midst of Samaria and Galilee. Then as He entered a certain village, there met Him ten men who were lepers, who stood afar off. And they lifted up their voices and said, "Jesus, Master, have mercy on us!" So when He saw them, He said to them, "Go, show yourselves to the priests." And so it was that as they went, they were cleansed. And one of them, when he saw that he was healed, returned, and with a loud voice glorified God, and fell down on his face at His feet, giving Him thanks. And he was a Samaritan. So Jesus answered and said, "Were there not ten cleansed? But where are the nine? Were there not any found who returned to give glory to God except this foreigner?" And He said to him, "Arise, go your way. Your faith has made you well" (Luke 17:11-19).

When I read this story, I regularly have to shake my head in amazement.

We do not see Jesus thoughtlessly walking past the lepers. Here were people who for weeks, months, and perhaps even years had not been allowed to keep social contact with the "normal citizens," for the law prohibited them from doing so because of their contagious illness. Medically, they were incurable. They lived off the beaten track in caves and tombs. They had no way of making a living. There were no possessions they could call their own. They received food from kind and compassionate family members and acquaintances, who day by day set out food in front of the tombs, which they then consumed far away from their loved ones. It was a struggle for survival in isolation and rejection as well as mental anguish.

What went through their minds when they saw Jesus from a distance and were not allowed to approach Him? Had they already heard of Jesus and that He did miracles and healed people? Perhaps they had been hoping for a long time that Jesus would visit their area? Did they summon up all their courage to draw attention to themselves because they had nothing to lose anyway? Were they already looking death in the eye and setting their last spark of hope in Jesus?

The text leaves us in the dark in this respect. We only read about how Jesus responded to them. Jesus told them to show themselves to the priests. Surprisingly, they did not hesitate and left immediately. They did not falter, nor did they doubt Jesus' command. They could have presented Him with all kinds of excuses as to why they could not go because they had leprosy. They could have quoted biblical passages to spiritually reinforce their passivity. They could have told Him that they were incapable; anyone would have understood.

No, they didn't do any of that. They didn't make any excuses. They went off, as Jesus had commanded. And in a miraculous way, their efforts and courage were rewarded. As they did what Jesus told them, they were healed from their leprosy. They experienced the glory of God and Jesus had initiated it.

As they did what Jesus told them,
they were healed from their leprosy.
They experienced the glory of God
and Jesus had initiated it.

But then we read about the strangest reactions. One of the ten ran back to Jesus, full of gratitude, and bowed down before Him and honored Him. But what about the other nine? We don't know! We don't read anything more about them.

One came back, the others did not. Why did only this one come back? Was he more desperate than all the other lepers? Had he been exposed to the shame, rejection, and pain of leprosy much longer than all the others? Had he experienced humiliations that the others had not, and was therefore more overwhelmed by this gift of grace? Here, too, we can only make assumptions. But what we do know is that ten ran to be healed and one ran further and was saved. Ten experienced God's glory in the form of signs and wonders, but one was not satisfied with this and ran after the greater glory, a glory that blessed him with earthly well-being and secured his eternal salvation.

Ten were desperate enough to be healed by Jesus, but only one was grateful enough to be saved. Ten experienced the glory of God, but only one pushed on into greater glory, the glory of salvation. Ten experienced a glory that is exclusively of earthly benefit, but only one progressed to the next level of glory and secured his eternal happiness, a glory of earthly and heavenly perfection.

Ten went and experienced glory, but only one went from glory to glory.

Signs and wonders are certainly God's glory. But salvation is undoubtedly more than that—it is greater glory.

EXPERIENCING GOD

In the last chapter, we read about the ten lepers and how they received healing, through which they all experienced God in a miraculous way. But only one of them returned to Jesus to thank Him. This shows us that it is possible to encounter God and still not know who He is.

Every day, people all over the world experience the works of God, albeit without coming to a knowledge of the truth. Of course, there are hundreds of reasons why that might be so. Perhaps they overlook God in their circumstances or are so taken up with their own lives that they find it difficult to break out of this mindset. Possibly what holds them back or keeps them in uncertainty is their social background, religion, disappointments, struggles, or simply life itself. Experiencing God is often a starting signal for being willing to search for more of Him, but many do not know where to look and see little incentive or sense in it.

God, who "will render to each one according to his deeds": eternal life to those who by patient continuance in doing good seek for glory, honor, and immortality (Romans 2:5-7).

In the last almost 20 years I have observed how countless people were touched by God, how they were deeply touched—they experienced God (this was unmistakable)—only to in the end to move away from God again and return to their old lifestyle, so that the encounter with God faded and seems to have almost no echo in their memories. Even today it still saddens me when I think of these friends and brothers and sisters who were supportive of me and who are called to great works for the kingdom of God, but who ultimately decided not to continue to pursue glory and immortality.

Experiencing God is wonderful, but it does not necessarily change our lives. Not only my experiences of the last years have shown me this, but also many biblical characters. The decision to search for glory and immortality or for more of God and not to stand still and think that this is all God has to offer is more influential than the experience of God that preceded it. An experience is by no means the end—rather, it is the beginning, the start, the point of entry, the door, and the access to an incredible journey in the companionship of a supernatural God in a seemingly ordinary world. The decision to actively search for it is the key to this venture.

SIMON, DO YOU LOVE ME?

I am infinitely grateful for the stories about Peter. They sound like a journey with ups and downs. Peter joins Jesus and then finds himself in the inner circle of the twelve apostles. He is the one who publicly confesses Jesus as Christ, only to be put in his place, being called "satan" just a little later. Then he positions himself in front of

Jesus when the soldiers come to capture Jesus only to deny Him in in front of the people a few hours later. He fled out of fear, but Jesus did not lose sight of him.

Fifty days after Jesus' resurrection, he stood up publicly with the rest of the apostles, preached the gospel, and led 3,000 people to faith. He performed miracles in the name of Jesus, was respected among the believers, but in his zeal he also sometimes made decisions that even caused Paul to confront him.

His life is so human and yet so encouraging, because if God can use Peter, then He can use each one of us.

We find a special story in John 21.

After these things Jesus showed Himself again to the disciples at the Sea of Tiberias, and in this way He showed Himself: Simon Peter, Thomas called the Twin, Nathanael of Cana in Galilee, the sons of Zebedee, and two others of His disciples were together. Simon Peter said to them, "I am going fishing." They said to him, "We are going with you also." They went out and immediately got into the boat, and that night they caught nothing (John 21:1-3).

Peter was close to Jesus for three and a half years without interruption. He saw at close quarters all the miracles that Jesus performed and could see for himself the power that the Son of God had. He saw Jesus heal people who had been hoping for healing for decades and raise someone who had already been dead for four days. Jesus walked on water, stilled the storm, defeated death—and Peter was a firsthand witness to it all.

After the resurrection, Jesus had already shown Himself to the disciples twice; they knew He was alive and was indeed the Messiah, the Christ, God Himself. But instead of turning the world upside down and conquering it, we read that Peter is going *fishing*—and not only that, but he also entices the others to go fishing too.

Instead of turning the world upside down and conquering it, we read that Peter is going fishing.

What's the matter, Peter? You know the mission, you know what to do, you must be convinced that from now on nothing is impossible. But no, they're going fishing. They are back in everyday life. They were fishermen before they met Jesus, and they returned there after Jesus was gone. Of course, they didn't catch a single fish all night.

In the further course of John 21, Jesus appears to them for the third time. When Peter recognizes Him, he leaves the boat, trudges through the water, and has a wonderful conversation with

Jesus. This is one of the best-known stories, which reveals God's boundless hope, love, and mercy. Three times in this conversation Jesus asks Peter, "Simon, Simon, son of Jonah, do you love Me?" and Peter answers, "Yes, Lord, You know that I love You." Then Jesus replies, "Feed My sheep," or "My lambs." But the third time Peter becomes sad.

We have only one word for *love*. In Greek there are four words for love: *agape, philia, storge,* and finally *eros. Agape* is the love of God, the love with which God loves people and with which people love God. It's a sacrificial and selfless love. *Philia* is brotherly love, a love that describes loyalty between friends but is not a sacrificial love like *agape. Eros* is physical and sensual love. *Storge* is instinctive love, similar to that between parents and children; it is a natural connection.

Here, it is fascinating to see which words were used in the conversation between Peter and Jesus. Jesus asked Peter if he loved Him with *agape* love. Peter replied that he loved Him, but he replied with the word *philia.*

Peter walked and lived with Jesus. He saw all that Jesus did and was one of the first to testify of Jesus' resurrection. He learned from Jesus and had been drawn to and touched by Jesus. The risen Lord spoke to him in a physically perfect condition, although He had been beaten, pierced, and crucified days before. If that didn't convince him, then what would?

Jesus asks him if he is now ready to love Him with divine, sacrificial, and selfless love, to follow Him, and to glorify God. Of course, we expect an emphatic yes, but unfortunately it was not so. While Peter had been touched, had experienced God, and was standing here before the Son of God who defeated death and lives, he could only answer Jesus in terms of *philia* love. What he felt was not *agape*; it was *philia*, brotherly love. On the one hand this is almost incomprehensible; on the other hand we learn that simply "experiencing God" does not necessarily transform us. Fantastic and almost unbelievable encounters and experiences with God give us no certainty that we really get to know God.

That is why Jesus gave us a mission: to preach the gospel to all creation, to lead people to salvation, to baptize them, and to make them disciples. Truth must be proclaimed by those who have not only experienced God but know who He is. God calls us to lead people from the experiential presence into the personal presence and to instruct them in a personal relationship with Jesus and set them free for that.

How then shall they call on Him in whom they have not believed? And how shall they believe in Him of whom they have not heard? And how shall they hear without a preacher? And how shall they preach unless they are sent? As it is written: "How beautiful are the feet of those who preach the gospel of peace, who bring glad tidings of good things!" But they have not all obeyed the gospel. For Isaiah says, "Lord, who has believed our report?" So then faith comes by hearing, and hearing by the word of God (Romans 10:14-17).

Truth must be proclaimed by
those who have not only experienced
God but know who He is.

JOB AND HIS FRIENDS

For a long time, the Book of Job was like a sealed book to me. Somehow, I had trouble understanding it. I could appreciate the beginning and the end—an interesting insight into the work of satan and how even the devil is under the authority of God, and that he wants to destroy God's servant. It describes Job's reward, because he clung steadfastly to God, although it seemed as if God had long since forsaken him. What an example and encouragement to cling to the Creator, knowing that ultimately the end of the story will always be rewarding and successful.

I found Job's four friends Zofar, Bildad, Elifas, and the young Elihu challenging—not because they were totally wrong—on the contrary, I even think their statements and justifications are good and partially really justifiable. I think they were truly people who shunned evil and tried to do good. Their arguments are quite plausible and seem correct, but in Job's case simply did not correspond to the truth.

These friends remind me very strongly of us Christians—we experience God in some areas and, unfortunately, we can still be totally wrong about the truth. We read a book on a certain topic or get great inspiration and then think we can apply this revelation to all possible areas or judge every situation through it, but life is often much more complex than that. We evaluate situations of fellow Christians, about whom we know nothing, just because we have received a revelation in one area of the kingdom and think we know where something is wrong. Just like Job's friends. And of course, it may be that the arguments are right and helpful to many, but in Job's case they were totally wrong, just as we are often wrong in our overzealousness.

The friends experienced God in their lives, for they definitely could claim a certain amount of understanding for themselves, but they did not know God, for they were totally wrong in their assessment of Job's situation.

THE HOUSE OF GOD

God reveals Himself to people in many different places, but He established a special place where people get to know Him. For this reason, God still asks us today, "Where is the house that you will build Me? And where is the place of My rest?" (Isa. 66:1).

God longs for a house of God, and this thing is the church or, better said, the *ecclesia*. This is the place that God has chosen for His special presence, for His resting place. It is a framework in which people meet God, learn the truth, and are changed. In the house of God, people are guided into a personal relationship with God, who was previously unfamiliar to them. In the church they are transformed, receive joy, live in light through fellowship, and are strengthened for the work of God in their lives and for the kingdom of heaven.

In the fellowship of the saints, as the Bible calls it, God releases inspiration, passion, longing, His gifts, and hunger. We infect one another with divine fire, care for those around us, live out the mission of Jesus, and glorify God. In this fellowship we push back the enemy, we penetrate heaven through our prayers, we bind the enemy with iron chains, and prepare the way for the King of Glory, the Almighty God, King Jesus.

If you have already experienced God, that's wonderful. But you really want to know God. Excellent! Your heart is burning for a personal encounter with God. Tremendous! Whether you have already experienced Him consciously or not, is not relevant here, as that alone has no dramatic effect on your future.

But if today you decide to seek God with perseverance, whether you have already experienced Him consciously or unconsciously and if it is your intention to continue seeking God even after the glorious encounters that you will have, then even heaven will not be able to prevent you from experiencing far more glorious things.

Ask, and it will be given to you; seek, and you will find; knock, and it will be opened to you. For everyone who asks receives, and he who seeks finds, and to him who knocks it will be opened (Matthew 7:7-8).

Ask! Seek! Knock! Do all this with perseverance, and you will receive more than you can wish and hope for. You will find things you weren't even looking for. You will have areas opened up to you that you didn't even know existed!

The kingdom of God is waiting for us! Come and experience greater glory.

KNOWING GOD

The previous levels of glory—creation, signs and wonders, and encountering God, along with the fourth level, that of knowing God—are based almost exclusively on God's action and our reaction. Despite our limited participation, God makes it quite easy for us to experience these levels of glory. Sometimes it happens in spite of ourselves, and at other times it requires only a small action on our part, for example, our confession, faith, or obedience.

From the fifth level onward, much more is required of us, and I will say more about that later.

I assign faith, salvation, water baptism, and baptism in the Holy Spirit to this (fourth) level.

We could perhaps even make further divisions to the many stages of glory, but to me they seem plausible and in the correct order as I have presented them. Another possibility would have been to list grace as one of the levels of glory. In the end, I could not assign grace to any one position. This led me to the decision to leave grace out of the list as it is unmistakably of paramount importance and essential for each level. Grace is part of each of the stages mentioned and without it none of the glories is attainable for us. The same is true of love.

Many of the glories overlap and fuel each other, and previous levels are very often, but not always, mandatory for moving on to a higher level. But every level of glory undoubtedly depends on the grace and love of God and is not accessible without them.

As a Christian, I enjoy the presence of God every day. Enthusiasm grips me when I remember and know that I am a child of God, that I can experience God and am surrounded by Him. I cannot claim to have known Him from childhood—not at all; apart from some well-known biblical stories, I was not familiar with the Word of God. But this did not detract from my desire and interest to experience more of God.

I can remember that when I was a child, I soaked up stories of miracles, answers to prayers, supernatural encounters, and extraordinary preservations and was amazed at them. It seemed to me as if everyone had a story to tell that they knew of or had heard from someone.

Could I experience that as well? Or what would I have to do to persuade God to delight me with the same surprises? Such thoughts were very familiar to me as a child. I didn't have faith that it would happen, because I thought I wasn't special enough for it, but I definitely had a certain hope—could I perhaps one day see an angel or would Jesus appear to me personally? Oh, how wonderful that would be!

However, these thoughts evaporated over the years; somehow, I was carried along by the typical maelstrom of life as a teenager. I never lost my faith in God, but I was increasingly interested in what the world had to offer. My two main passions were soccer and girls. Soccer was supposed to help me become wealthy and, finally, to attract more girls. Yes, I believed in God, but I didn't know how to believe God.

How could I build this personal relationship and level that I didn't even know about then—believing in a God, making my decisions according to His guidance, and giving myself fully to Him? Drawing near to Him so that He draws near to me? How could He become for me a personal God and Father and not just an imaginary being that I heard was somewhere up there in heaven, while I had nothing to do with Him otherwise?

FAITH

As already mentioned, Friday, March 16, 2001 would become the day that changed everything and turned my life upside down. In the personal presence of God, I met a personal God. He overwhelmed me, took hold of me, and captivated me. Nothing would ever be the same again. Suddenly this God, who had seemed so far away, came so incredibly close to me. I couldn't possibly deny this meeting with God. God said it was time for me to get to know Him—and what an incredible journey I have been having to this day. It was the day on which I firmly decided in faith to become a child of God; I invited Jesus into my heart, and He did not hesitate but immediately began His work in me.

> But as many as received Him, to them He gave the right to become children of God, to those who believe in His name: who were born, not of blood, nor of the will of the flesh, nor of the will of man, but of God (John 1:12-13).

Yes, we are all God's creatures and of course He does not deprive any of us of His love. Everyone can meet God personally. But not all are children of God. This privilege is given to those who receive Jesus Christ into their hearts in faith. Those who confess Jesus as Lord are justified by God and enabled by Him to live according to the faith and confession. Eternity belongs to them; they receive eternal life and are connected to the Almighty God, whom, as His children, they also call Father.

> That if you confess with your mouth the Lord Jesus and believe in your heart that God has raised Him from the dead, you will be saved. For with the heart one believes unto righteousness, and with the mouth confession is made unto salvation. For the Scripture says, "Whoever believes on Him will not be put to shame." For there is no distinction between Jew and Greek, for the same Lord over all is rich to all who call upon Him. For "whoever calls on the name of the Lord shall be saved" (Romans 10:9-13).

Only with salvation does this intimate and personal relationship with and to God open up to us. An incredible journey awaits you, from faith to faith. In your personal relationship with God you will get to know Him as Father, as provider, healer, teacher, answerer of your prayers, as strength, peace, love, truth, light on your path, and so much more. He does not withhold anything from us as long as we develop hunger for more. But the most wonderful thing about it is that in this relationship we not only learn a lot about God—no—we become personally and intimately acquainted with God. For what is the point of knowing a great deal about God if one day we depart from this world but do not know God Himself?

He does not withhold anything from us
as long as we develop hunger for more.

The ten lepers are an excellent example of the glory levels two to four. All ten experienced the glory of signs and miracles in the form of the healing they received; they had, of course, in the presence of Jesus also experienced God. But only one returned, as he was the only one who had come to know God, and gave Him glory or *doxa*, as it is called in Greek, so that in the end he was also saved. Ten experienced God and were healed, but only one knew God and received eternal salvation.

John wrote in John 1:14 that Jesus, the Word of God, lived among them, and all saw through and in Him the glory of God, but although thousands saw this glory, it was not recognized by all for what it was. Despite the immense and glorious miracles that Jesus performed and were witnessed by so many people, according to the Acts of the Apostles, there were only 120 or just over 500 left after Jesus' resurrection who recognized Him as the promised Messiah, Son of God, and God (see 1 Cor. 15:6).

All should come to know God and experience Him personally—that is clearly God's passionate desire.

BAPTISM IN WATER

He who believes and is baptized will be saved (Mark 16:16).

Several times a year I travel to Asia to speak at conferences, strengthen and send out pastors, teach Bible students, and help with church development projects, among other things. Despite the sometimes immense dangers that Christians experience in this part of the world, their urgency in taking the Gospel to the most distant places is in no way diminished. It seems that in their suffering, they even receive boldness, become stronger through persecution, grow in faith through dangers, and increase in number when oppressed. These wonderful Christians are the heroes of the faith of our time and the reason why Christianity is growing enormously in the Asian regions. They do not only believe in God, they believe God and place themselves at His disposal as His feet and hands in a lost world, and God rewards them with success, but also with an eternal treasure in heaven.

*They do not only believe in God, they believe
God and place themselves at His disposal
as His feet and hands in a lost world,
and God rewards them with success,
but also with an eternal treasure in heaven.*

It is not unusual to find people in India, Nepal, or Myanmar who believe in Jesus. Even at evangelistic events there are hundreds and thousands of Hindus who confess Jesus as God. There is no doubt that great seed is being scattered here. However, we should not ignore the cultural aspects—some registers attribute to India and Hinduism more than three hundred million gods. To believe in Jesus in these regions does not necessarily mean to worship Jesus exclusively. Thoughts like, "If you already have ten gods in your life, it can't hurt to add Jesus as the eleventh," are not unusual.

But people who really have come to know God do not stop merely at confessing their faith. They are baptized in water—and that is exactly where the problems and difficulties often begin. Baptism is an outward sign and confession for the exclusive faith in Jesus Christ. But it is not simply a sign of our faith. In baptism we communicate to the whole visible and invisible world that we confess only Jesus as God and turn away from all other gods and deities.

People who, for example, profess Christianity in India are ostracized by their Hindu relatives after baptism; they are persecuted, harassed, and sometimes killed. They understand the power and message of baptism. With the conscious decision to be baptized in water, we expressly set an end to our past life with its gods, sins, and misconduct. It is assimilated into the death of Jesus so that at the same time we are enabled to receive a new and eternal life. This is done through the glory of the Father.

Therefore we were buried with Him through baptism into death, that just as Christ was raised from the dead by the glory of the Father, even so we also should walk in newness of life (Romans 6:4).

Our identity from now on is in Christ and in no other god. Our life has been made new and we can live a new life (see Rom. 6:1-10). In baptism, we confess that there is no other God except the Father, Son, and Holy Spirit.

BAPTISM WITH THE HOLY SPIRIT

For John truly baptized with water, but you shall be baptized with the Holy Spirit not many days from now. …But you shall receive power when the Holy Spirit has come upon you; and you shall be witnesses to Me in Jerusalem, and in all Judea and Samaria, and to the end of the earth (Acts 1:5, 8).

After my salvation I was in a spiritual "land of milk and honey" for about two months; I was in a bubble and totally overwhelmed by God. I devoured the Word of God and prayed, sometimes for hours.

I tried to spend every free minute with like-minded people, singing worship songs with them, praying in the name of Jesus, and talking about the God who does miracles.

All this happened during preparation for my school-leaving exams, and as you can imagine my final grades suffered quite a lot as a result. I'm not proud of that, of course, and I would advise everyone to do things differently, but I certainly would not want to trade this time for anything else. Not that I would necessarily have obtained better grades, because you really couldn't say that I was very diligent. Well, to be honest, I was pretty lazy at school, and in fun I often say, "Either they had mercy on me with my exams or they were sick and tired of me and wanted to get rid of me."

I remember the oral examination in religious education, when I shuffled into the room and tackled the questions. I stood at the front of the room full of zeal and full of the Spirit, as I thought, and was totally convinced of my performance. Religious Education had always been one of my strong subjects, and now as a born-again Christian, it could not be anything other than outstanding.

After answering the questions and surviving the time of waiting in the school corridor, I was called into the classroom to get my grade. I was sure it would be a high score, at least 12 points, more likely 13 or 14 and even 15 would not be unrealistic.

And then the moment came. The three teachers had come to an agreement. As a reward for my oral examination, I, who had encountered God personally—and with my lecture I would certainly have gone down well with large crowds—was given…three points. *What?* Three points? Yes, a subsidiary course in religion—topic failed. "Who cares about the topic," I thought to myself, "the lecture was epic"; God was sure to be satisfied with me. Maybe God was, but unfortunately the examiners weren't; they assessed the contents and I failed the exam.

Today I am thankful for that because I was allowed to learn early that my life in this world does not automatically turn out well, even if I am full of faith. Work and commitment are still part of it; indeed, they are even a testimony and confirmation of my faith.

After two months, the first euphoria slowly but surely subsided, and suddenly everyday life seemed to catch up with me again. On the day of my salvation I threw my cigarette package into the trash can and had no desire for these cigarettes in the weeks that followed, but the addiction came sneaking back—and not only the addiction, but also other things in my life that were not pleasing to God. Had I not left them behind?

What was happening? Was I slowly losing my faith or falling away from God again? I tried to fight it with all my might, but the harder I tried, the deeper I slid back again. It started with smoking, then it was relationships with women, and I almost took drugs for the first time in my life. It was so strange—after all, I loved God, still longed for Him, He was more real to me than ever before, and yet all these carnal pleasures overpowered me and seemed to enslave me to pull me into a current that was even stronger than prior to my salvation, and I had no idea how I could stop it.

I cried out to the Lord, wept because I was sorry, repented countless times, tried to turn back, and felt guilty because I could not do it. But then salvation came—one night in August 2001, I had a dream, and in this night vision God revealed the solution to me.

In this dream I was in a large hall filled with thousands of people. They had all come to attend a competition. In the middle of the hall there was a table, which two persons approached, standing facing each other ready to compete against each other in arm wrestling. I was in the middle of the crowd watching the events from a distance.

A giant of enormous stature defeated one opponent after another with uncanny ease, knocking out his opponents and shaming them. No one seemed even remotely able to compete with him. Toward the end of the event, the giant had no more adversaries. He waited for a while and hoped for another courageous challenger.

I thought to myself, *Who would be so stupid as to compete against this monster? It can only end in disgrace.* Of course, there was no one who wanted to challenge the giant, but as he became more and more impatient, he took a microphone and asked for someone in the hall to arm-wrestle him, no matter who. Of course, nobody responded, so he picked his own opponent and pointed his finger in my direction: "You!" I looked around—who did he mean? Was it possibly me? Yes, it was me!

Oh, how embarrassing, I thought to myself, *this can only end in a thrashing.* But unfortunately, there seemed to be no way out for me; I had to face the situation. So I walked through the crowd toward the podium and joined the giant. We faced each other, I stretched out my arm; my opponent had a huge paw and my hand was completely swallowed up in his. The referee did the countdown, and when he yelled "Go!" I closed my eyes hoping this thing wouldn't end in a total debacle.

After a few moments I was surprised, because nothing was moving. When I then opened my eyes, I was totally amazed to see this giant, red in the face, trying to defeat me, but he could not do it. My arm was not moving even a fraction of an inch. Euphoria and hope spread through me and I saw my chance of leaving the hall cheering over a magnificent victory.

I tried to focus all my strength to defeat this seemingly overpowering rival. But as hard as I pressed, the hand of this monster moved as little as mine. Suddenly it rose up from inside of me: "Holy Spirit, help me"—and in a flash I pushed the hand of the giant onto the table like a child's hand and he experienced a crushing defeat!

The whole hall froze in shock, there was no sound to be heard, and a little later it was filled with jubilation, inebriation, and frenzy. People ran toward me; they took me on their shoulders and carried me around. I tried to reassure them and repeated again and again— it wasn't me, it was the Holy Spirit. It has nothing to do with me; it was the Holy Spirit.

I didn't win, it was the Holy Spirit.

Then I woke up and knew immediately: The solution for all my struggles is the Holy Spirit.

It wasn't me, it was the Holy Spirit.

I had heard of the baptism with the Holy Spirit, and some people in my prayer group were already speaking in new tongues, so I expressed my desire for baptism in the Spirit. A short time later, at a prayer meeting, I was baptized with the Holy Spirit and began to speak, pray, and praise God in new languages. I received power that would change my struggles and my life once and for all. Smoking was now a thing of the past; addictions and immorality were eradicated from my everyday life one after the other.

Did I still have to struggle with difficulties, temptations, and lusts afterward? Yes, I did. Sometimes there were days when it was no problem at all, but there were also times that were hard. The only difference was the Holy Spirit; I submitted myself to Him and let Him lead the fight. Since then I have gone from victory to victory. Every fight I won led me to greater freedom. Every time I overcame something, it made me stronger and the sin in my life weaker.

Together with the Holy Spirit I am still fighting against the kingdom of darkness and the flesh in which I live, but I know that the fight has already been won by Jesus, and with the Holy Spirit I cannot lose.

Each time he said, "My grace is all you need. My power works best in weakness" (2 Corinthians 12:9 NLT).

To be baptized with the Holy Spirit and to speak in new tongues is simply amazing. Not only do we allow God to work through us and in us by doing so, we also change the atmosphere just as we do through prayer.

Shortly after my baptism with the Holy Spirit, I prayed very much in new tongues, and today this is still a large part of my everyday life and prayer life.

Around the turn of the millennium, Croatia experienced a strong revival in the Holy Spirit. I took part in some events and was also privileged to be able to help with some of the organization. During this time, the largest halls were booked and filled to capacity for charismatic events. Signs and miracles were a matter of course, demons manifested regularly, and people were set free.

At one meeting, I was seated in a row with people who had experienced strong demonic attacks in their lives and were still being tormented by these impure spirits. I sat calmly in my seat and prayed inwardly in tongues without making a sound or moving my lips. Suddenly the woman next to me turned around, rolled her eyes backward, and asked me in a deep male voice not to pray in tongues anymore, as she could not endure it. It was not the person speaking, but a demon, who is a spirit and can discern atmospheres. These and many other experiences confirmed to me the power of the baptism in the Holy Spirit and the power of speaking in tongues.

It is not just an option that we have; I am convinced that salvation, water baptism, and baptism in the Spirit belong together in knowing God Himself and His power and leading a wonderful life filled with God.

Salvation, water baptism, and baptism in the Spirit belong together in knowing God Himself and His power.

Jesus said in John 14:12, "Most assuredly, I say to you, he who believes in Me, the works that I do he will do also; and greater works than these he will do, because I go to My Father." These works are there to glorify God the Father (verse 13). And directly after this statement Jesus speaks about sending the other helper, by whom He meant the Holy Spirit.

I am convinced that we receive the Holy Spirit at salvation, just as the disciples were filled with the Holy Spirit shortly after Jesus' resurrection (see John 20:22). But only with the baptism in the Holy

Spirit did they receive the strength to continue the works of Jesus in authority, boldness, and with signs and wonders.

Surprisingly, the first miracle of the apostles after Jesus' ascension to heaven is described in Acts 3—a man who had been lame from birth was carried daily to the gate of the temple to beg. We don't know for how many years he had been sitting there every day, but it is very likely that Jesus passed by him every now and then. And here are Peter and John, who did not give alms to this man, but healed him with authority and boldness. They simply continued the works of Jesus because they had received power with the baptism in the Holy Spirit.

Baptism with the Holy Spirit is not a phenomenon restricted to Pentecostals or charismatics; it is a gift of God for all who believe and are willing to do the same works as Jesus did and even greater ones.

Salvation is such a wonderful gift—it is eternal life for all who believe in Jesus Christ and gives us the certainty of being redeemed and having received the forgiveness of sins.

Water baptism is not only a symbolic act; it is a powerful proclamation to the visible and invisible world that one has turned away from all gods and belongs solely to, and worships, the true God—the Father, Son, and Holy Spirit.

Baptism in the Holy Spirit is the power to continue the work of Jesus in spreading the kingdom of God on earth—to make the one true God known throughout the whole world so that heaven may be brought to earth.

Get ready for a life full of adventure with an almighty God. He will lead and accompany you from grace to grace, faith to faith, and glory to glory. He is a personal God who longs for a personal relationship with you. Respond to this offer, and God will break open the restrictions of your life forever.

LEVEL 5

SEEING GOD

"A man cannot see God," "We cannot see God," "God is invisible," or "Nobody has ever seen God"—these are only a few statements we sometimes hear and which I have also made myself. All these statements are also true and can be confirmed by passages from the Bible, and yet they do not reflect the whole truth. For we read again and again of people in the Bible who tell us, "I saw the Lord," "I stood in heaven and saw one sitting on the throne," "I saw the Lord standing," "I saw the form of the Lord." I found more than 80 people who saw and looked at God in one way or another.

But how could that be possible when even the Bible says:

No one has seen God at any time (1 John 4:12).

Seeing God has to do with the levels of glory. Not everyone was exposed to the same degree of glory as Enoch or Moses. Adam and Eve could see God before the Fall in a way that Jacob, for example, could not, even though he said at Penuel, "I have seen God face to face."

The word *face* in Hebrew is *panim*. It is mainly translated as a singular word, but in Hebrew it is plural. This indicates a higher number than one; God has many faces and He cannot present each one to all people, even if He would like to.

**God has many faces and He cannot
present each one to all people,
even if He would like to.**

This may sound confusing, but we humans have a similar situation. So, on the one hand I am the father of my son and many people can observe me in this role, but others will never experience the closeness and love I give to my child. On the other hand, my child, as much as I love him (and my father's heart would like to lay the world at his feet), will never be able to experience me as a husband, for that is reserved exclusively for my wife. My son can observe what I am like as a husband, he can learn many qualities of a husband from me, but the intimacy I share with my wife in secret will never be experienced by anyone else, nor should it be.

Jacob saw God's face, but it was not as glorious as the unity with God that Adam and Eve experienced.

Other people who saw God were:

Moses

My servant Moses; he is faithful in all My house. I speak with him face to face, even plainly, and not in dark sayings; **and he sees the form of the Lord** (Numbers 12:7-8).

Isaiah

In the year that King Uzziah died, **I saw the Lord sitting on a throne, high and lifted up,** *and the train of His robe filled the temple* (Isaiah 6:1).

David

O God, You are my God; early will I seek You; my soul thirsts for You; my flesh longs for You in a dry and thirsty land where there is no water. **So I have looked for You in the sanctuary,** *to see Your power and Your glory* (Psalm 63:1-2).

Job

I have heard of You by the hearing of the ear, but **now my eye sees You** (Job 42:5).

Amos

I saw the Lord *standing by the altar, and He said...* (Amos 9:1).

Jacob

So Jacob called the name of the place Peniel [Penuel]: ***"For I
have seen God face to face,*** *and my life is preserved"* (Genesis
32:30).

Daniel

*I watched till thrones were put in place, and the Ancient of Days
was seated; His garment was white as snow, and the hair of His
head was like pure wool. His throne was a fiery flame, its wheels
a burning fire* (Daniel 7:9).

John

*Immediately I was in the Spirit; and behold, a throne set in
heaven, and One sat on the throne. And He who sat there was
like a jasper and a sardius stone in appearance; and there was
a rainbow around the throne, in appearance like an emerald*
(Revelation 4:2-3).

Moses, Aaron, Nadab, Abihu, and the 70 Elders

*Then Moses went up, also Aaron, Nadab, and Abihu, and
seventy of the elders of Israel, and they saw the God of Israel.
And there was under His feet as it were a paved work of sapphire
stone, and it was like the very heavens in its clarity. But on the
nobles of the children of Israel He did not lay His hand. So they
saw God, and they ate and drank* (Exodus 24:9-11).

FAITH, AND THEN? SANCTIFICATION

The experiences mentioned differ from each other. We could also explore them more closely and explain in more detail how these encounters happened. Whatever they were like, we know this—it was a wonderful level of glory. It is more intense than experiencing or knowing God. This is the next step to which God wants to lead you; He is preparing you for a deep and groundbreaking encounter with Himself.

When God leads you into this realm of glory, you will look back on your past life and suddenly realize that in the light of this new glory you barely knew anything about God before. Job 42:5 is the best illustration of this experience for me—there was no one in the whole world who was like Job, righteous and upright, who feared God and avoided evil (see Job 1:8). Even God boasted to His angels about His servant Job, and He was not disappointed because even in the darkest hours that life sometimes brings, Job did not turn away from God.

He was undoubtedly a hero of faith who could not explain the dramas of his life and, at times, wavered but never doubted God. In the end, God rewarded Him with a new level of glory, whereupon Job proclaimed:

I have heard of You by the hearing of the ear, but now my eye sees You (Job 42:5).

Do you believe in Jesus? Wonderful! But don't think of it as your final state. Salvation is the goal for the lost, but it is no longer your goal, for you already belong to God's eternal family. God still has special things for you; He wants to show you more of Himself and His glory. He will take you by the hand and guide you in His ways so that you may experience greater glory. The next path is sanctification.

And there I will meet with the children of Israel, and the tabernacle shall be sanctified by My glory (Exodus 29:43).

The prerequisite for knowing God is and remains faith; seeing God, on the other hand, is reserved for those who allow themselves to be sanctified.

Seeing God is reserved for those who allow themselves to be sanctified.

In the ears of many, sanctification is a very unpleasant word. They equate it with restrictions and with the loss of fun and pleasure. It's like having to part with everything that gives you pleasure. Does a joyful temperament have to be exchanged for a serious and lifeless expression of sanctification? Nothing could be further from the truth. God Himself sits on His throne and laughs, and in His presence there is fullness of joy (see Ps. 2:4; 16:11).

Is sanctification sometimes unpleasant? Of course, it is, like so many things in life. People do sports to stay in shape and that's not always pleasant, but it's worth it. Many people subject themselves to cosmetic treatments so that they look better, and plucking the eyebrows is the most pleasant of them, although even that is painful. Others even go under the knife in order to get closer to their ideal of beauty, and they accept the pain involved—just to mention a few things.

But sanctification is not so much like drill in the army as it is preparation for the encounter with the person we adore. It is the preparation for our walk to the altar and the first meeting with the bridegroom. The weeks and months beforehand are not only stressful, but we have butterflies in the stomach.

A bride goes to the beautician, to the bridal gown show, and voluntarily even sheds a few pounds so as to be in the best possible condition for meeting her groom. There are weeks of abstinence and often detailed organization, and many other things are neglected because they are less important. It's an intensive time, which is worthwhile because this special day is constantly before her eyes.

On the night before the special day, the bride cannot sleep. For days she has hardly eaten for excitement. The last hours feel like an eternity, her stomach rumbles continuously, her feelings are about to explode in all directions. Seconds feel like minutes, and hours like eternity.

Thousands of thoughts race through her head. Doubt and anticipation, powerlessness and feelings of happiness, weakness, and security—a real chaos that she probably won't remember once she stands in front of him, the bridegroom.

And then this long walk to the altar—the moment you've longed for for so long. In an instant everything is forgotten; nothing else seems important anymore. All worries, hardships, and stress are gone in one fell swoop, and suddenly the past seems so distant because the glory of this encounter and the joyful expectation of the future with its radiance put everything else in the shade.

The glory of this encounter and the joyful expectation of the future with its radiance put everything else in the shade.

For me, sanctification is more like this scenario than the rebuke, instruction, and discipline in military training. When God takes us by the hand and sanctifies us, He still does so as a loving Father and never as an authoritarian or selfish dictator.

But to experience this level, sanctification is imperative, just as God asked Moses to sanctify the people because He wanted to show Himself to all the Israelites in a way in which they had not yet seen Him.

Then the Lord said to Moses, "Go to the people and consecrate them today and tomorrow, and let them wash their clothes. And let them be ready for the third day. For on the third day the Lord will come down upon Mount Sinai in the sight of all the people" (Exodus 19:10-11).

God wants to show Himself to you so that you can say like Job, "Now my eyes have seen Him." On the way to this glorious experience, keep Hebrews 12:14 as close to your heart as possible.

Pursue peace with all people, and holiness, without which no one will see the Lord (Hebrews 12:14).

Sanctification is essential in order to see God; without it, it is not possible.

SEVENTY-FOUR PEOPLE AT A BANQUET WITH GOD

I have been reading the Bible passage in Exodus 24:9-11 for almost 20 years now, and these three verses still fascinate me in a way that hardly any other passage in the Word of God does.

You have to realize what a glorious event took place here. Not only did 74 people experience the living God, they were even allowed to see Him. But not only that, at the same time they had permission to take one step further into the glory: *they beheld God.*

I don't know if you've just understood this as a simple piece of information or if you have a certain immunity to biblical stories and can absorb certain biblical events with little emotion, but this experience of the 74 people should spark something in our hearts. Think about it—Moses and Aaron, and Aaron's eldest sons Nadab and Abihu, as well as the 70 elders of Israel, took part in a banquet prepared by God with His angels—and *they saw God!*

This was no vision, or dream, or prophetic inspiration. What we read here is also not a pictorial representation that requires further interpretation. What is written here is exactly what it also means— they saw God with their physical eyes, and it was not ecstasy, rapture, or a trance. There is also no need to consider whether this was a purely emotional or spiritual experience. What these 74 individuals experienced with God was just as real as the fact that you are holding this book in your hand.

Maybe now you are asking, "But Hrvoje, why are you already classifying this level of glory here? Could anything be more glorious than that? Is not only heaven itself more glorious?" Those are exactly the thoughts I had over the years about this wonderful event. Was there anything that could be better or more desirable? Until I studied Second Corinthians 3:18 a little more carefully.

But we all, with unveiled face, beholding as in a mirror the glory of the Lord, are being transformed into the same image from glory to glory, just as by the Spirit of the Lord (2 Corinthians 3:18).

The decisive factor and measure of glory is not exclusively the event itself and how glorious it seems. The verifiable unit of measurement is transformation. How much has the level of glory changed me? And that means "into that same image." In other words, the glory experienced is measured by how much I have become more like Jesus.

The glory experienced is measured by how much I have become more like Jesus.

If we apply this standard, then it is logical that I have not defined this glory as being at a higher level.

As wonderful as this experience was for the 74 people, the transformation was minimal.

Why do I think that? We just have to read on and see what happened around 20 or 30 days later among the people of Israel, and 73 of these 74 persons (everyone except Moses) were at the center of it and were responsible for it.

Now when the people saw that Moses delayed coming down from the mountain, the people gathered together to Aaron, and said to him, "Come, make us gods that shall go before us; for as for this Moses, the man who brought us up out of the land of

Egypt, we do not know what has become of him." And Aaron said to them, "Break off the golden earrings which are in the ears of your wives, your sons, and your daughters, and bring them to me." So all the people broke off the golden earrings which were in their ears, and brought them to Aaron. And he received the gold from their hand, and he fashioned it with an engraving tool, and made a molded calf. Then they said, "This is your god, O Israel, that brought you out of the land of Egypt!" So when Aaron saw it, he built an altar before it. And Aaron made a proclamation and said, "Tomorrow is a feast to the Lord." Then they rose early on the next day, offered burnt offerings, and brought peace offerings; and the people sat down to eat and drink, and rose up to play. And the Lord said to Moses, "Go, get down! For your people whom you brought out of the land of Egypt have corrupted themselves" (Exodus 32:1-7).

After the banquet God had provided, the Lord called Moses farther up the mountain to discuss the next steps with him. The remaining 73 rejoined the people and told them that Moses had continued to go higher into the presence of God. I can only imagine the enthusiasm with which the elders told of their experiences.

But perhaps 20 or 30 days later, when there was no sign of life from Moses far and wide, the people became impatient. They assembled before Aaron and requested him to make them gods.

After everything that the Israelites had experienced with God, they were set on being unfaithful to Him! They had seen how God had fed them daily in a supernatural way. They had witnessed God dividing the sea with His finger so that they could walk through it on dry land. When Egypt experienced the ten plagues, God held His protective hand over Israel so that they would not be affected, although they lived in the same region. And many other miracles. Whatever was going on inside of them, none of the glorious miracles had changed them in such a way that they now clung to their God.

After everything that the Israelites
had experienced with God,
they were set on being unfaithful to Him!

And now they had this desire to worship man-made gods, who were to rule over them—that makes no sense at all! How can a created being like man form a creature that is divine and can protect him? And this proposal came from people who had experienced God's majesty and holiness! They had seen how unapproachable and mighty God is, and yet they wished for deaf-mute idols that had ears and mouths and yet did not hear or speak.

As incomprehensible as this story seems to us, Aaron's reaction is even more astounding. This was the high priest of Israel, who together with Moses had overseen the exodus of Israel from Egypt and had convinced the people about God; this was the brother of Moses, to whom God had granted the privilege, along with 73 others, of seeing greater glory; this was someone who had seen God and had eaten and drunk with Him—and while it seems insane, Aaron accepted the people's proposal as if it were a matter of course.

Aaron asked the people to gather gold, everything they could find, in order to melt it in the fire and make it into an idol, a golden calf. Aaron completed his work, and I would like to believe that in the meantime he had undergone conviction regarding his deed. Perhaps he still wanted to remedy the situation and turn it around, and that was why he called the calf "Yahweh"—he gave it the wonderful name of God, possibly to set his own mind to rest. But it was too late, for he was right at the center, and the situation had got out of hand.

Verse 6 of chapter 32 sounds almost like enjoyment—the people stood up to amuse themselves. Other translations write *they stood up to play*, while others replace "play" with "dance." But the scene was not at all as harmless as it seems; *The Living Bible* says more aptly: "afterwards they sat down to feast and drink at a wild party, followed by sexual immorality." The various translations are based on the Hebrew word *sahaq*, and its meaning is undoubtedly erotic and sexual in nature. For example, *sahaq* is used in Genesis 26:8 when Abimelech saw Isaac and Rebekah and deduced their true relationship status from their intimate togetherness. It also describes in Genesis 39:17 the accusation of sexual harassment with which Joseph was wrongly confronted (after which he was imprisoned).

Not only did the Israelites turn away from God, they held orgies to give free rein to all their carnality and sinfulness. And right at the center—Aaron, Nadab, Abihu, and the 70 elders! They did not take a stand for God against the people, although they had seen God with their own eyes; on the contrary, they were just as guilty.

How did this happen? Just 20 to 30 days before they had seen God as only a few people had. The experience was still totally present. Yes, it was, but measured by the change by which the extent of God's glory can be assessed, there must be more glorious levels still.

Why did the Israelites fail all along the line? I'm convinced it is because of a lack of the fear of the Lord. And that is precisely the next level of the glory of God that we will explore in the following chapter.

THE FEAR OF THE LORD

For the next five levels, as with the previous ones, God alone is sovereign, and of course we can't claim any responsibility here. But in order to experience and push through to these levels, we are expected to do more than just react. The value of these glories is too holy, too precious, and, yes, it demands a price from us. Not because we could contribute anything to glory through our actions, but God wants to see if we are ready to risk everything when we have found the greatest treasure—Jesus. Then God rewards us with higher levels of glory.

> *Now when He was in Jerusalem at the Passover, during the feast, many believed in His name when they saw the signs which He did. But Jesus did not commit Himself to them, because He knew all men, and had no need that anyone should testify of man, for He knew what was in man* (John 2:23-25).

Many people believed in Jesus, but He did not entrust Himself to all of them. Do you want to be someone in whom Jesus confides? Then leave everything behind and follow Him, as His apostles did, whom He took into His confidence.

It's not a very popular message these days, but the reward won't be the same for everyone. Yes, salvation is something that all believers will have in common. But this is not the case with the reward, which will correspond to our work here on earth, the nature of which will be revealed by the fire of God.

Now if anyone builds on this foundation with gold, silver, precious stones, wood, hay, straw, each one's work will become clear; for the Day will declare it, because it will be revealed by fire; and the fire will test each one's work, of what sort it is. If anyone's work which he has built on it endures, he will receive a reward. If anyone's work is burned, he will suffer loss; but he himself will be saved, yet so as through fire (1 Corinthians 3:12-15).

At this level of glory, we are no longer satisfied with salvation, redemption, and signs and wonders, even if this is more than we have ever deserved. And if salvation was the only thing that Jesus had bequeathed to us, it would of course be far more than we have ever deserved.

But because Jesus has given us so much more, because He is so wonderful and perfect, because He is worthy and because He is God, I do not want to be content with salvation but want to advance to further levels of glory so as to place the world at the feet of my Lord Jesus. I want to realize what a wonderful treasure I have found in Jesus and therefore be ready to give everything for it.

Again, the kingdom of heaven is like treasure hidden in a field, which a man found and hid; and for joy over it he goes and sells all that he has and buys that field (Matthew 13:44).

With your faith and salvation, you have already received a treasure; on the next five levels of glory there are more incredible treasures, but they require everything we have. Is that frightening? It should not be, because Jesus promised us a hundredfold harvest even in this time (see Mark 10:30).

**Because He is so wonderful and perfect,
I do not want to be content with salvation but want to
advance to further levels of glory so as to place
the world at the feet of my Lord Jesus.**

WHAT IS YOUR GREATEST WISH?

Once when I was again reading the story of Solomon and about how God appeared to him in a dream with a question and a lucrative offer, the Holy Spirit asked me what my choice would have been. I immediately thought of dozens of wishes, but in this case there was only one. So it should be well thought out. Because I have been consciously following Jesus for almost 20 years—and from the very beginning it was my heart's desire and yearning to serve and please Him—I have come as far as to say that material things are not important enough for me to sacrifice such a wish for them.

As a Christian I thought of things like faith, peace, revelation, passion, or love. All these made perfect sense, and I definitely can't have enough of them.

But because I had only one wish, I had to think it over. What would be the best thing for advancing the kingdom of God and giving God the greatest possible glory?

Finances are good in themselves and make it possible to build children's homes or women's shelters, hospitals, community buildings, schools, and much more. With finances, we could implement projects that we have on our hearts. We could create change in economically weak areas. The possibilities with sufficient finances seem endless.

But the heart of human beings seems to have its difficulties with vast amounts of material goods and tends to fall in love with money, and the love of money is the root of all evil. No, it is not finances. It has to be something that will allow God to bless me totally, but at the same time also protect me from setting my heart on money.

Maybe it is faith? Faith can move mountains. The Bible says, "all things are possible to him who believes." That sounds great, because without faith it is also impossible to please God. The Bible talks about faith countless times; a vast number of books have been written about it, but would I choose faith?

After careful consideration, I concluded that it was not faith. Please don't misunderstand me. Faith is wonderful, and I need much more of it. But I am concerned about the fact that people get used to faith and after a while it is no longer regarded as anything special; they even turn away from it and sometimes even fall away from it, although they have experienced the goodness of God so clearly in their lives. No, I don't need faith, I need something that makes faith grow in me. Something that prevents me from taking faith for granted. Something to protect me from losing my faith. That's what I'd choose if I had a wish.

But what is that? Is it revelation, perhaps? I thought about that, too. If I saw more of God, if I knew more about Him, if God revealed Himself to me and I learned more about Him, wouldn't that be wonderful? So is revelation what I would choose if God asked me what I wish for?

I thought about Exodus 24:9-11, because for me this is one of the most incredible stories and experiences that anyone can have with God. God called Moses to the mountain. His brother Aaron, Nadab, Abihu, and the 70 elders of Israel joined him. The Bible says that they saw God and ate and drank with Him.

That really wows me. I really get goosebumps when I think about it. What more can there be than seeing God? That's what you want as a believer; it seems to be the final goal; can there be anything better? I would love to jump up and scream like a football commentator after the deciding goal has been scored in the final,

"That's it, that's it!" That's all there can be. There's nothing more emotional than that.

But is that really what I would choose? The problem is not this experience we read about; it's truly exceptional. As I mentioned in the previous chapter, the frightening part came afterward when the leaders of Israel, who had seen this wonderful God with their eyes and had eaten and drunk with Him, a short time later raised the golden calf and worshiped it as God and Savior. What? That can't be true! To have such an experience and then to turn away! What you shouldn't think was possible really happened. Probably not more than 20 to 30 days after their encounter with God they betrayed Him. After such a revelation of God, they still did not remain faithful to Him.

We also see Adam and Eve, who saw God day after day and spent all the days of their lives with Him—and they too were unfaithful to God.

No, when I read about these events in the Bible, I have to say—I love and need revelation, but I would not choose it either. There must be something that allows me to see God and meet with Him, but without my denying Him or becoming unfaithful to Him. That's what I would choose. But what is it?

As wonderful as it is to see God—this level of glory that I am seeking is one level higher; it is the foundation for the next four wonderful levels of glory. What is it? Is it wisdom, as Solomon chose? Oh, wisdom is wonderful, and I can't have enough of it, but despite his wisdom Solomon distanced himself from God in his later years. So it can't be wisdom either. It must be something that, despite wisdom and understanding, keeps me humble and does not let me forget that without God I am nothing.

What about love? It must be that, right? It's the greatest gift of all! But then I remembered the words of Jesus who told us that the love of many would grow cold. I said, "God, I certainly need more love, but more than that, I need something that will not let my love grow cold."

Then I wondered who I could or would ask. It would have to be someone who is already old, who loves God, has experienced and seen many things, who has witnessed God's goodness and love, who has overcome difficulties and even dramatic experiences.

I thought of people I knew or had read about, people who were still alive or had long since passed away. I thought of individuals from Bible history, from Abel to John the apostle. In the end, it seemed somehow obvious and wise to me to ask Solomon. Apart from Jesus of course, but as He was the One asking me the question, I first left Jesus out of the picture, out of the competition so to speak.

What would Solomon advise me? The King of Israel, who ruled over a kingdom unlike any other and who had no easy start in life as a child, but was chosen by God and his father. He had to resist the opposition of his brother until he was finally crowned and acknowledged as king. He found favor in the eyes of the Lord, who also added wealth and fortune to his wish. Solomon saw the favor and glory of the Lord, and yet he departed from God. He allowed his heart to lean toward other gods and thus deviate from God's laws and ordinances.

What would Solomon recommend to me or what did he teach us at the end of his life? And then I read it in Ecclesiastes:

Let us hear the conclusion of the whole matter: Fear God and keep His commandments, for this is man's all (Ecclesiastes 12:13).

I WISH FOR THE FEAR OF THE LORD

It is the fear of the Lord! Yes, I'd choose that and definitely prefer that to anything else. The fear of the Lord keeps my faith to the end; it keeps my love glowing; it makes revelations flow, and it is the beginning of wisdom.

The fear of the Lord keeps my faith to the end;
it keeps my love glowing; it makes revelations flow,
and it is the beginning of wisdom.

Fearing God has nothing to do with being afraid. Rather, it is respect, reverence, esteem, admiration, and acknowledgement. It is the awareness of how limited, imperfect, and mortal we are in the face of an immortal, almighty, and perfect God.

When we walk in the fear of the Lord, then we do not look at how and whether we can get through with certain attitudes and lifestyles. In the fear of God there is the desire to please God, to walk in His ways, and to do His will. Fearing God means living in humility, selflessness, and holiness, and also recognizing how dependent we are on this great God.

The word *fear* or *reverence* is used over 300 times in the scriptures in connection with God. Awe is the natural reaction when God meets us in a glorious way or when we find ourselves at a higher level of glory.

And when I saw Him, I fell at His feet as dead. But He laid His right hand on me, saying to me, "Do not be afraid; I am the First and the Last" (Revelation 1:17).

Even John the apostle, who did not leave Jesus' side for more than three years and did not shrink from the danger of death even during the crucifixion of Jesus. He was the only one there in the worst hours of his Rabbi. He belonged to the innermost circle of Christ, had a special place in Jesus' heart, and was one of three who saw Jesus shine on the Mount of Transfiguration. He experienced the resurrection and ascension of Jesus firsthand and saw it with his own eyes. Despite these experiences, and although he knew and worshiped Jesus like almost no one else, John also fell down in awe before Jesus when He appeared before him in greater glory.

The fear of the Lord is our natural reaction when we encounter higher levels of glory. It is true—we are the righteousness of Christ, and the old has passed away and the new has come; I no longer live, but Christ lives in me. That is the most wonderful truth. But when the glory appears on such an extraordinary scale, then we fall on our faces and confess that we are merely sinners who, without God, are only a heap of misery.

When the glory appears on such an extraordinary scale, then we fall on our faces and confess that we are merely sinners who, without God, are only a heap of misery.

IT IS NOT A GIFT

God wants to give us the fear of the Lord, but it does not come cheaply. It is not transmitted by laying on of hands or received by a miracle. The fear of God is learned. It requires time, our commitment, and our attention. It demands sacrifice and self-sacrifice.

> *Come, you children, listen to me; I will teach you the fear of the Lord* (Psalm 34:11).

The fear of the Lord is the door to unbelievable heights and depths in God. It is the gateway to favor with God and men. A gateway to blessings we never even dared to dream of.

There is nothing in the entire Bible that is associated with more promises than the fear of the Lord—neither faith, grace, or trust, nor prayer, fasting, or the Word of God. Even love is not linked to as many promises as the fear of God is. It is my rock-solid conviction that the fear of the Lord unlocks every promise! Because if we have the fear of the Lord, there is nothing else we can lack.

Here is a small list of the blessings associated with the fear of the Lord:

- It reverses want (Ps. 34:9).
- God draws us into His confidence (Ps. 25:14).
- The fullness of the covenant is applied (Ps. 25:14).
- It helps us not to sin (Exod. 20:20).
- God hears our voice (Mal. 3:16).
- He always works for our good (Deut. 6:24).
- It allows us to live well and happily (Ps. 128:2).

- It generates wealth and riches (Ps. 112:3).

- It gives wisdom (Ps. 111:10).

- It enables us to have a successful marriage (Ps. 128:3).

- It brings blessing to our descendants/children (Ps. 112:2).

- It releases the blessing of God (Ps. 128:4).

- It prolongs the days of our life (Prov. 10:27).

- It pours out endless mercy upon us (Ps. 103:17).

- It brings healing (Mal. 4:2).

- It gives us comfort (Acts 9:31).

- It dispels worries and creates trust (Prov. 14:26).

- It enables us to receive revelation (Ps. 25:12).

- It brings salvation (Ps. 145:19).

- It enables me to recognize evil (Prov. 3:7).

- It creates security (Ps. 16:8).

- It secures our harvest (Jer. 5:24).

- It gives us a place of refuge (Prov. 14:26).

- It edifies us (Acts 9:31).

- It is a source of life for us (Prov. 14:27).

- It gives a hope far beyond death (Ps. 112:3).

- Prayers are answered (Heb. 5:7).

- It activates angels (Ps. 34:7).

- It makes us sleep content and satisfied (Prov. 19:23).

- It is protection from evil (Prov. 16:6).

- It gives us peace (Acts 9:31).

- It gives deliverance from enemies (2 Kings 17:39).

- It is a light in darkness (Mal. 4:2).

- It comforts us (Job 4:6).

- It creates in us a generous heart (Acts 4:32).

- It makes the church grow (Acts 9:31).

- It gives us honor (Prov. 22:4).

- What we say is heard in heaven (Mal. 3:16).

- It makes our righteousness endure forever (Ps. 112:3).

- It gives the earth to our descendants (Ps. 25:13).

We could add pages to this list, because in the fear of the Lord there is "all-inclusive" blessing. When God sees the fear of the Lord, He holds nothing back from us; it is the threshold to God's treasures and His immeasurable wealth, both spiritual and natural.

WHAT THE CHURCH FATHERS SAY ABOUT THE FEAR OF THE LORD

Gregory the Miracle-Worker, also called Thaumaturgus, was a bishop and church father in the third century. He believed the fear of the Lord was the mother of all virtues.[1] With this understanding and this attitude, which was based on the fear of the Lord, he began his ministry in the third century in the bishopric of Neocesarea on the Black Sea. When he took office, there were only 17 Christians in the whole city. Because of his God-fearing life, the kingdom of God spread extremely fast in his city, and one inhabitant after the other was added to the church until on the day of his death there were only 17 unbelievers left in the whole city.

St. John of Antioch from the fourth century, also called Chrysostom ("golden-mouthed"), said about the fear of the Lord: "If we have the fear of the Lord, we lack nothing, and if we do not have it, then we are poorer than all men, even if we had a kingdom." He continued: "We will acquire this; we will give everything for it! And if we also had to sacrifice our life, if we had to have our bodies cut to pieces, we would not hesitate."[2] In order to gain the fear of the Lord, it is worth giving up everything.

In an address about the fear of the Lord in the fourth century, Ephrem the Syrian said, "Because these holy men feared God, the creatures feared them and obeyed their commands. The one who fears the Lord is above all other fears and leaves all the horrors of the world far behind him. He is far from all fear; no fear ever comes near Him when he fears God and observes all His commandments."[3]

We cannot have a better foundation in life than the fear of the Lord. When you begin your day, begin it in the fear of the Lord and give honor and glory to God. If you are an employee at work, then work with the attitude of the fear of the Lord and try to give of your best. If you are part of a local church, be a blessing and a living stone in God's temple who fears the Lord, and you will bear much fruit.

If you need breakthroughs and answers to prayer, always begin with the fear of God. Before focusing on your own concerns, turn your gaze away from your needs toward God, your Creator. If you are called by the Lord to ministry or to plant a church, always make the fear of God the foundation of the ministry.

Our calling is important, but the kingdom of God is more important. If you want to see success in your life and your daily experience, make the fear of God the protection for your habits. And the work of your hands, the words of your mouth, and the fruit of your ministry will be blessed.

God will undoubtedly take care of the fruit, growth, and success. He will secure it, humiliate your enemies, and increase your property. You will lack nothing, and even more than that, He will meet your needs with the riches of His glory (see Phil. 4:19).

Your prayers will not be unheard, but a prayer in the fear of the Lord is accompanied by the attitude, "Not my will be done, but Yours!" The fear of the Lord wants to spread the kingdom of God and not our own.

The fear of the Lord wants to spread the kingdom of God and not our own.

Abraham was asked to sacrifice his son—and in the moment when he raised his hand to kill Isaac, after he had laid him on the altar and tied him firmly to it, the angel of the Lord called to him from heaven and spoke:

"Abraham, Abraham!" So he said, "Here I am." And He said, "Do not lay your hand on the lad, or do anything to him; for now I know that you fear God, since you have not withheld your son, your only son, from Me" (Genesis 22:11-12).

We know Abraham as the father of faith. In faith he left his family and set out for a land he had never seen before and which he did not know, but which God had promised to him, a God who was unknown to him and his family, but whom he believed and whose voice he followed—and God counted it to him as righteousness (see Gen. 15:6).

But to give up the most precious thing in life takes more than faith; it takes the fear of the Lord. Before this, Abraham was already the father of faith who had left everything and trusted God, but when he was prepared to sacrifice his son, it became apparent that he feared God. Nothing was as dear to his heart as his God, not even the most precious thing he had. That is the fear of God.

The fear of God is shown first and foremost in the place God occupies in our lives. He is the source of our life, the origin of our worship, and the end of our praise. We submit our worries to him, come before Him with thanksgiving, give Him honor and our attention every day, and when we lose ourselves in everyday life, we return to Him.

It is amazing how a shepherd boy named David, in faith and with a slingshot, a few stones, and God, defeated as a matter of course the ten- to twelve-foot-tall Goliath, of whom all Israel was afraid (see 1 Sam. 17:26-40). But when he was overcome with sorrows and fears, he fled from King Saul, who was just two meters tall and insane. Overwhelmed with fear, he did not seek out his slingshot but was satisfied only with the sword of Goliath; he did not seek refuge in God but thought he could find it in the camp of the enemy, with the Gittites (see 1 Sam. 21:9). Abandoned, lonely, and facing an uncertain future, he ended up in a dark, dirty cave called *Adullam*. Adullam means "retreat" or "refuge," and it was there that David wrote Psalm 34.

I will bless the Lord at all times; His praise shall continually be in my mouth. My soul shall make its boast in the Lord; the humble shall hear of it and be glad. Oh, magnify the Lord with me, and let us exalt His name together. I sought the Lord, and He heard me, and delivered me from all my fears. They looked to Him and were radiant, and their faces were not ashamed. This poor man cried out, and the Lord heard him, and saved him out of all his troubles. The angel of the Lord encamps all around those who fear Him, and delivers them. Oh, taste and see that the Lord is good; blessed is the man who trusts in Him! Oh, fear the Lord, you His saints! There is no want to those who fear Him (Psalm 34:1-9).

Fearing God does not mean being immune to everyday life. Struggling with worries, fears, and uncertainty is part of life. But to fear God means to come before God with these attacks, to turn our gaze on Him, and to allow God to correct our point of view.

When we fear God, we honor, exalt, and worship Him; we skip time for things in everyday life in order to draw near to the Lord. We base our decisions on His pleasure. Not only with our words but with our life we communicate the message—God is my number one, and I owe everything to Him. *He who fears God laughs and is confident, for those who fear Him have no lack* (see Ps. 34:9).

If we stray from the right path, we return to God because we fear Him. When we find ourselves in a dead end, we turn to God and ask forgiveness for forgetting to include Him in our decisions. When we seek financial solutions by working even more, at the expense of our time with God, then we turn back in faith and reflect on Him. That is how we live in the fear of the Lord.

Those who fear the Lord are not perfect, but they are on their way to being made perfect. A saint who fears the Lord is not without sin and error, but he cannot live in peace with sin. He seeks God and is transformed more and more from glory to glory. He becomes more and more like Jesus. This is the fear of the Lord, and we need it more than ever.

Develop a hunger for the fear of God and make it your priority and desire. Always remember what Solomon said: "Let us hear the conclusion of the whole matter: Fear God and keep His commandments, for this is man's all" (Eccles. 12:13).

If you have the fear of the Lord, then you will lack nothing, absolutely nothing, whether spiritual, physical, emotional, or material. God will prove Himself in every area. He will open His treasuries for you, and the way to greater glory will not be hidden from you. You will experience breakthroughs and multiplication on all levels of your life.

PRAYER

Lord, teach us the fear of the Lord.

Open our eyes to the precious and immeasurable glory of the fear of the Lord. Let us realize what a wonderful quality the fear of the Lord is, perhaps even the greatest thing in the world. With the fear of the Lord, we flee from a narcissistic world, and instead of constantly reciting our requests to You, which You do not forget in Your love and mercy, we make it our priority to please You.

Our King, more than anything, we want to exalt You in worship, reverence, admiration, enthusiasm, devotion, awe, and desire. Open our hearts wide to the fear of the Lord. Lord, teach us to fear God. We ask this in Jesus' name.

NOTES

1. Gregorius Thaumaturgus, "Praise to Origen," qtd. in O. Bardenhewer and Th. Schermann, *Bibliothek der Kirchenväter: Eine Auswahl patristischer Werke in deutscher Übersetzung* (Dionysius Areopagita), Kempten and Munich, 1911, 35 (Dionysius, 245).

2. John Chrysostomus, "Commentary on the Letter to the Philippians, Fourth Homily," qtd in O. Bardenhewer and K. Weyman, Ibid. (Johannes Chrysostomus, Vol. VII), Kempten and Munich, 1924, 55.

3. Ephrem the Syrian, "Address concerning the fear of the Lord and the Last Judgment of God and the Last Day," qtd. in Ibid. (Ephräm der Syrer, Volume I), Kempten and Munich, 1919, 67.

LEVEL 7

WALKING WITH GOD

Well over 80 people were permitted to see God, but the Bible describes only a little more than a handful of them as people who walked with God.

Enoch, Noah, Abraham, Isaac, and Levi walked with God, all of them great personalities who changed the face of the world with their lives. Of most of those who saw God, we do not even know the names, but of those who walked with God, the names will be known to man and heaven for all eternity.

Seeing God can be an extraordinary and sometimes unique event that we remember throughout our whole life. It's an experience that shakes us to the core and which we can draw on until the end of our lives. Such encounters with God's glory are important; they are not always emotional and stirring, but always groundbreaking and radical.

In our home, God has a central and vital role; He is the one around whom our lives chiefly revolve. For us, God is not imaginary, but a real and authentic person.

Our son is growing up in this environment, and prayer, Bible reading, missions, preaching, outreach, fasting, giving, angels, the supernatural, and reflecting Jesus in our everyday lives—all this is quite natural to him in regard to what it means to be a Christian, because this is how we live. He loves Jesus and intentionally chose to be baptized with the firm decision to follow Jesus the whole way.

And yet every evening I pray for him that God will prepare his heart for a groundbreaking personal encounter with Him, a meeting with God that will ignite his heart to such an extent that he will not simply remain a believer but will live out his calling with passion right to the end. I pray for an encounter to walk with God in the fear of the Lord. Before the Almighty he will not be able to lean on my faith; I can only help him and serve as an example he can follow, so he can run way further than I ever did.

Without his own personal encounter with God, his faith would only develop into a religion adorned with tradition, which would lose all its strength.

SET APART BUT NOT CUT OFF

So all the days of Enoch were three hundred and sixty-five years. And Enoch walked with God; and he was not, for God took him (Genesis 5:23-24).

Enoch was the first person about whom the Word of God says that he walked with God. He was 365 years old when God took him away. Interestingly, a year has 365 days and it is not difficult to see the connection—walking with God is not a rendezvous agreed for a certain time, a day, or a week; it is a continuous and daily life with God. He is not consulted only when major decisions are to be made or when we find ourselves in critical and, perhaps, hopeless situations; this is a relationship in which we give more attention to walking in His ways than to involving God in our own ways. This request then becomes a lifestyle 365 days a year, just as Enoch lived it out.

This is a relationship in which we give more attention to walking in His ways than to involving God in our own ways.

To experience signs and miracles, to experience God, to recognize Him, and to believe in Him—these are not exclusive indicators of whether someone walks with God. But they are prerequisites for living on the seventh level of glory.

To walk with God, as Enoch, Noah, and Abraham did, you need the fear of the Lord—you are so deeply touched by God that it seems impossible for you not to align your life exclusively with God.

There are different levels of glory; one of these is "walking with God," and this is not simply a gift of grace from God. Of course it is without doubt a gift of God's grace, and we cannot earn it, and yet we must prove ourselves worthy to enter it by means of our lifestyle and conduct. You set yourself apart for God, you are willing to sacrifice comforts and even make uncomfortable decisions that do not necessarily seem to be to your advantage, but which are God's will—and that is perfectly sufficient for you.

As you know how we exhorted, and comforted, and charged every one of you, as a father does his own children, that you would walk worthy of God who calls you into His own kingdom and glory (1 Thessalonians 2:11-12).

We are called to God's kingdom and glory. Our Father in heaven does not want to withhold anything from us; He has legally granted us the inexhaustible riches of His glory through Jesus Christ. When we truly respect and fear God with our whole being, then we will walk worthy of God and gain access to higher glories.

CLASH OF CULTURES

We do not read or learn very much about Enoch in the Bible. We can only imagine what it was like for him and in what kind of environment and world he lived.

The first humans, Adam and Eve, had to leave the greatest possible glory because of their transgression and settle east of the Garden of Eden. Then Eve gave birth to two sons—Cain and Abel. The story of what happened between these two blood relatives ended dramatically. In a buildup of jealousy, dissatisfaction, and envy, Cain killed his God-fearing brother Abel. Cain then had to flee from the face of God and settle in a lower realm of glory.

After the expulsion from paradise, this was already the second downward step within two generations. In chapters four and five of the Book of Genesis we read of two bloodlines—the descendants of Cain and the descendants of Seth, another son of Adam and Eve, whom the Lord gave to them after the murder of Abel. Cain's lineage belongs to the seed of the serpent (see 1 John 3:12); it is godless humanity and a society characterized by materialism, egoism, sodomy, godlessness, envy, brutality, contempt for mankind, and murder. Seth's descendants in turn are their opposite—they are the God-fearing lineage.

And as for Seth, to him also a son was born; and he named him Enosh. Then men began to call on the name of the Lord (Genesis 4:26).

In the time of Seth, people began to call upon God. Unlike Cain's descendants, they did not take the side of the serpent but aligned themselves with God. These two bloodlines or lineages were in conflict with each other and it seemed that the side of darkness would triumph—in the tenth generation we already read that Noah was the only righteous person left.

Enoch grew up and lived out his faith in the context of this clash and conflict of cultures. He had to consciously decide to follow the

Lord and walk with Him. While Enoch lived in the world, he was not of the world. His thoughts, emotions, and lifestyle were directed toward the eternal God and not toward the transient pleasures of the world. That does not mean that Enoch was a religious freak, but just that he didn't allow himself to be overwhelmed by the zeitgeist and held on to the ways of God in a twisted world.

CALLED TO INCREDIBLE DEEDS

Noah was another hero of the faith who walked with the Lord.

This is the genealogy of Noah. Noah was a just man, perfect in his generations. Noah walked with God. And Noah begot three sons: Shem, Ham, and Japheth. The earth also was corrupt before God, and the earth was filled with violence. So God looked upon the earth, and indeed it was corrupt; for all flesh had corrupted their way on the earth (Genesis 6:9-12).

Children and adults alike are fascinated by the story of Noah and the flood. It has been controversially discussed thousands of times, but even most scientists who are unfamiliar with the Bible describe a dramatic flood that spread across the earth a few millennia ago.

Only Noah and his family, eight people in all, were saved from this ecological disaster. However, that was only possible because Noah obeyed the voice of God and did not conform to the lifestyle of that period. Noah did not live for the pleasure of the moment; he was resolved to sacrifice himself for the glory of eternity.

Consider this: Noah heard something from God that nearly everyone else probably doubted—that it would start raining in 120 years, and that water would flood the whole earth. To help us understand this, the first mention of rain is in Genesis 7, verses 4 and 12. It seems that before that day something like rain was unknown to humankind.

If that is true, and no one had ever seen water fall from heaven before, it would have been absurd to believe Noah. Maybe everyone around him thought he was out of his mind. But then Noah started a unique construction project that would take him 120 years to complete. An incredibly big boat, an ark—in an area far away from the oceans.

In those days, which were corrupt and filled with violence, mockery at Noah's expense seemed to be a given. A maniac, a laughingstock, for whom his whole family was ridiculed. But what farsightedness Noah had, what faith, and what devotion in the face of all this doubt and the zeitgeist!

It is costly to become worthy of this level of glory. You have to lose your life to find it. Noah lost his life because he dedicated himself to a "fantasy project" day in, day out, for 120 years.

---

*It is costly to become worthy of this level of glory.
You have to lose your life to find it.*

AND YET BELIEVE

Abraham, the father of faith, was another hero of faith who walked and lived his life consistently with God.

And he blessed Joseph, and said: "God, before whom my fathers Abraham and Isaac walked" (Genesis 48:15).

Abraham, of course, symbolizes faith, but also the fear of the Lord and selflessness. How else can it be explained that he clung to God, who had promised to give him a land in which he would ultimately remain as a stranger until his death?

By faith Abraham obeyed when he was called to go out to the place which he would receive as an inheritance. And he went out, not knowing where he was going. By faith he dwelt in the land of promise as in a foreign country, dwelling in tents with Isaac and Jacob, the heirs with him of the same promise; for he waited for the city which has foundations, whose builder and maker is God (Hebrews 11:8-10).

He left his familiar surroundings and embarked on an uncertain journey. During his lifetime he was never able to settle in this foreign land that God had promised him. He had to travel and lived in tents as a Bedouin. Children and grandchildren were born to him and God blessed him with fertility and success, but he did not live to see the conquest of the land. Abraham sacrificed himself for a promise that would not be fulfilled until long after his death well over 400 years later.

The father of faith did not live a life for personal gain at all, although he experienced prosperity in many areas precisely because of this attitude, but he gave his life for the following generations and yet had a fulfilled life in every respect. That's what it means to walk with God.

HIS PROPERTY

The priests of the tribe of Levi were other men of God who stayed at this level of glory.

> *My covenant was with him, one of life and peace, and I gave them to him that he might fear Me; so he feared Me and was reverent before My name. The law of truth was in his mouth, and injustice was not found on his lips. He walked with Me in peace and equity, and turned many away from iniquity* (Malachi 2:5-6).

The fear of God was also the foundation for the ministry and life of the Levites, the priestly tribe of Israel. The priests had a very special position in God's eyes—they were His property. That sounds wonderful at first—who wouldn't want to have special VIP status? As marvelous as that is, there are unique conditions for living at this level of glory. The priests were God's property and they were not allowed to own anything themselves. The people had received laws from the Lord, but the additional requirements for the priests were even stricter. All Israel was allowed to carry out its own business, but the priests were exclusively at the disposal of the people of Israel. Each man was responsible for himself and, at most, for his clan, but the priests were called to account for all Israel.

Yes, the priests had a special place and a unique role with God. They experienced the glory of God in a measure that was not granted to the rest of the nation, but in order to enjoy all these privileges they also endured great privations.

Yes, the person who walks with God and lives at this level of glory has risen above all egoism.

**When you walk with God, you are
different from the rest of the world.**

When you walk with God, you are different from the rest of the world. You're not just talking about love, you're living love. You do not just point out problems, you do something to change them, even when your commitment is not appreciated. Not only do you notice a need, you tackle it yourself and try to eradicate it. Desperation will only be a momentary situation for you, but your God is always a God of the impossible. You not only have compassion for your fellow human beings, you also feel responsibility. You are richly blessed, but an even greater giver. You reflect God with your life as the apostles did:

> *Now when they saw the boldness of Peter and John, and perceived that they were uneducated and untrained men, they marveled. And they realized that they had been with Jesus* (Acts 4:13).

The word for *uneducated* in this verse is the Greek word *idiotes*, which doubtless needs no explanation.

It seems quite clear how Peter and John were regarded by the rulers, priests, elders, Sadducees, and scribes—they laughed at them, and the image of the apostles was correspondingly scorned, to put it mildly. But one thing even these educated and highly esteemed people could not deny—the wisdom and understanding that flowed out of the mouths of these *idiotes* and fishermen was amazing. And then it became clear to them where this knowledge came from—they had been with Jesus and walked with Him.

When we walk with God, our advice and wisdom will not go unrecognized, even if we are evidently disdained. But in the end, we will be consulted by the world when it is in desperation, because nothing has changed about God's love for the world.

It's a privilege to walk with God.

LEARNING FROM THE HEROES OF FAITH

We can learn the following points from the heroes of faith who walked with God:

1. Keep to God's ways in a degenerate world.

2. Do not live for the pleasure of the moment but for the glory of eternity.

3. Do not seek only your personal blessing, but make decisions that will bless future generations.

4. Allow God to own you and use you for a lost generation.

THE FACE OF GOD

Adam and Eve lived in a perfect environment of the presence and glory of God. I call this level of glory "unity with God," and I will say more about this in the next chapter. Due to rebellion and sin, they were ultimately no longer able to live in this perfect environment, as certain levels of glory are incompatible with sin.

> *For all have sinned and fall short of the glory of God* (Romans 3:23).

Experiencing creation, signs and wonders, and God form one of the levels of glory with which all humankind is blessed without restriction. These are environments of the general grace of God, and even sin does not exclude people from it. However, they have a "date of expiry"—not a general one, but a personal one—and this is the length of your life on earth.

It is important to understand that these levels have no influence on eternal glory. Only from the level "Knowing God" is the endless and unlimited eternity and glory opened to us. Here the redeeming and transforming grace begins to work in the form of conviction of sin. From here on, sin no longer feels comfortable, because your spirit is resisting it together with the Holy Spirit.

Therefore, it was impossible for Adam and Eve to continue to dwell in the perfect glory, as the sin in them made them feel uncomfortable. They also hid from the face of God, which is yet another level of glory. (In most English versions, "face of God" is translated "presence of the Lord." The Hebrew word *paniym* literally means face, but is also rightly used in a great variety of applications like presence, countenance, or sight. Please note: in all following scriptures, where "presence of the Lord" is translated it is talking about the glory level "face of God.")

And they heard the sound of the Lord God walking in the garden in the cool of the day, and Adam and his wife hid themselves from the presence of the Lord God among the trees of the garden (Genesis 3:8).

CAIN AND ABEL

Cain and Abel, the children of Adam and Eve, also lived in an environment of glory—the "face of God." The first people had to leave Eden, the garden of God, because they had become unable and unworthy to live in this presence as a result of their sin and rebellion. But this does not mean that Cain and Abel were excluded from any presence of God; they were merely at a lower level of the glory of God.

Then Cain went out from the presence of the Lord and dwelt in the land of Nod on the east of Eden (Genesis 4:16).

Cain and Abel also lived in an environment of glory—the face of God. The story of these two brothers unfortunately ended tragically in a family drama, the elder killed the younger, and Cain followed the path of his parents, descending to the next lower level of glory. Sin and blood guilt made it impossible for him to continue living before the face of God. Humankind no longer dwelt in Eden, the perfect environment of God, and in comparison, everything that is less glorious does not seem like glory. But living before the face of God is still unbelievably glorious compared to the other levels.

The narrative about Cain and Abel shows us quite clearly the characteristics of this level of glory.

Now Abel was a keeper of sheep, but Cain was a tiller of the ground. And in the process of time it came to pass that Cain brought an offering of the fruit of the ground to the Lord. Abel also brought of the firstborn of his flock and of their fat. And the Lord respected Abel and his offering, but He did not respect Cain and his offering. And Cain was very angry, and his countenance fell. So the Lord said to Cain, "Why are you angry? And why has your countenance fallen? If you do well, will you not be accepted? And if you do not do well, sin lies at the door. And its desire is for you, but you should rule over it" (Genesis 4:2-7).

When we analyze this passage, we obtain some deeper insight into the situation and circumstances that otherwise might easily be overlooked. Cain was a farmer and Abel a shepherd—nothing unusual at first glance. The profession of arable farmer is probably much more physically demanding than that of a shepherd and appears to be the harder choice.

Both brothers bring offerings to God. They are aware of God's presence; they also know how to honor God with sacrifices—that is, to give up things that have a personal value. The Lord respected Abel's sacrifice, but there was something wrong with Cain's sacrifice. The text does not clearly say why this was, but it does not leave us completely in the dark either.

Abel brought a sacrifice from the "firstlings." It wasn't a normal sacrifice, but firstlings, as the Bible calls them. He took of the first animals that his flock had brought forth and presented them to God. Before he used anything for himself and took care of his own needs, he sacrificed to the Lord. His actions testify to great faith because he gave up the entire first "harvest" and trusted God for more. In Hebrews 11, Abel is mentioned as the forerunner of faith and the first hero of faith.

By faith Abel offered to God a more excellent sacrifice than Cain, through which he obtained witness that he was righteous, God testifying of his gifts; and through it he being dead still speaks (Hebrews 11:4).

Abel did not merely come before God with a sacrifice. His sacrifice was simply a natural expression of something much richer— his faith, his trust, his fear of the Lord. Nothing was more important to him than to show God how important He was in his life.

Nothing was more important to Abel than to show God how important He was in his life.

Meanwhile, Cain also brought a sacrifice. However, his gift was not a firstling, but after some time Cain brought an offering of the fruits of the ground to the Lord. His priorities and those of his brother differed considerably. "After some time" indicates a certain delay; it expresses a different process. Where Abel immediately thought of God at the harvest, Cain hesitated. He did not bring God the first and best, but only a selected remainder of his harvest. He kept the best and the first for himself; he dedicated it to his own enjoyment and consumption, but this is not worthy of the glory level "the face of God."

There is another amazing aspect to this story: Abel was a shepherd. Why did someone decide to take up this profession at that time? Being a farmer makes absolute sense—you work the field to have enough food. But a shepherd? It was only in the time of Noah and after the flood, nine generations later, that God granted the flesh of animals to man for food; before that it was forbidden. So Abel's motivation in choosing his career was not the greatest possible personal gain or wealth. Likewise, we can exclude the production of clothes, because with four living individuals there was no great necessity for this.

What motivated Abel to become a shepherd? We can discount personal concerns and needs. His desire to approach God and worship Him alone was expressed in his choice of profession. Nothing else was as important to him as honoring his God and staying in the presence of God. He chose a profession that enabled him to make sacrifices exclusively to God. There was no other purpose in his work.

Give to the Lord, O families of the peoples, give to the Lord glory and strength. Give to the Lord the glory due His name; bring an offering, and come before Him. Oh, worship the Lord in the beauty of holiness! (1 Chronicles 16:28-29)

PREPARED TO SACRIFICE

Sacrifice is required for coming before the face of God, and if we wish to dwell before the face of God, a sacrificial life is required. It's not cheap, but it's so unbelievable and incredibly wonderful.

We need people who are so deeply moved by God that they go from glory to glory with all that they possess and enter the glory level of the face of God—people and groups who are willing to lose everything to win the face of God.

Our nations and the world are waiting longingly for these heroes—heroes who are misunderstood, overlooked, underestimated, and rejected. And yet humankind is dependent on them—they stand in the gap for nations, they fight against the god of this world, they dethrone powers and principalities of darkness, they have a seat in the council of God and a voice in the courtrooms of heaven. They bring about justice and do not shrink from dangers.

They may be unknown, but the destiny of nations depends on them. They sacrifice their name, honor, and respect for the kingdom of God and in the name of God. They may seem unsuccessful, but many will owe their success to these heroes without knowing it.

These are not hyper-spiritual people who seem crazy because of their theology and are obviously lone warriors seeking recognition because they feel rejected. No, even if they have been rejected, they love unconditionally. Even if they get hurt, they forgive unreservedly. They may lose everything, but they don't lose their joy. In late old age they have wrinkles on their faces—not as a result of great worries, but because they laugh much and contagiously—and their faces, full of confidence, are always radiant. Just as Jesus' face was radiant— how could it be otherwise in the presence of God?

OFTEN ALONE, BUT NEVER LONELY

Sometimes you feel alone in this presence, but never lonely. People who enjoy the presence of God may seem to isolate themselves, but they actually long for more people who are willing to press on into this level of glory.

> *So the Lord spoke to Moses face to face, as a man speaks to his friend. And he would return to the camp, but his servant Joshua the son of Nun, a young man, did not depart from the tabernacle* (Exodus 33:11).

People who enjoy the presence of God may seem to isolate themselves, but they actually long for more people who are willing to press on into this level of glory.

Moses was in the presence of God and he had access to this presence, but there too he was alone. Personally, he enjoyed this area of glory, but there was no one else with whom he could share these experiences.

Moses certainly received incredible things for himself, but the main focus of glory was not Moses alone, but the people. He received instructions and wisdom to teach and guide Israel and to guide them in the ways of the Lord. The face of God is not a place to retreat to forever. Moses isolated himself for a time, but not because he wanted to escape from problems and natural responsibility, but so that he could finally return to the camp and to the people in order to solve the problems and remedy the grievances.

Remember Exodus 24 when Moses, Aaron, Nadab, Abihu, and the 70 elders saw God and ate and drank with Him on the mountain—a wonderful experience that they were privileged to have. A company of 74 people at the feast, they rejoiced and talked, ate and drank delicacies from heaven, and at the same time God was among them and was their center—what a feast! After this event, which they were all sure to have remembered until the end of their lives, the elders returned to the camp, but Moses did not go with them. He ascended in the opposite direction, climbing higher toward the top of the mountain, into the darkness, deeper into glory, and into the face of God. He went alone, without the feeling of loneliness.

Moses did not leave his companions just because they were not pursuing the same glory. Too many people today leave churches and their surroundings if they do not see the same fire in their Christian brothers and sisters. They don't think they are spiritual enough.

Of course, a change of church or a new environment can often be the right thing and important for many people, but unfortunately I have seen too many people who chase the spiritual peaks yet never become integrated into a local body, always with the argument that the church is not spiritual enough. Then they migrate from church to church, from conference to conference, constantly looking for a kick, and ending up being so "spiritual" that they are of no earthly use. Years pass and they still live in a bubble instead of going back to the camp, like Moses, to the people, to their fellow men in order to serve them, to see themselves as a part of the body of Christ, and to be an inspiration to others.

When you advance to this level of glory, you experience God in a miraculous way—on the one hand, you suddenly thirst for more of Him, and on the other you receive passion for people and are ready to stand in the gap for them and want to serve them.

MARKED

Seeing the face of God is not always accompanied by feelings of enthusiasm; we may also experience struggles and agonizing, as Jacob did at Penuel. He wrestled with God and the scar of this fight became a mark until the end of his life. He limped because of a damaged hip.

So Jacob called the name of the place Peniel: "For I have seen God face to face, and my life is preserved" (Genesis 32:30).

Please do not misunderstand me—physical limitations are by no means an inevitable consequence of this level of glory. But going from glory to glory cannot leave you unchanged. You will be changed, transformed, and marked. To press through to the face of God will mark you with something that is not necessarily associated with the presence of God—as with Jacob, who limped all his life.

With Moses, on the other hand, it was expressed in his face.

Now it was so, when Moses came down from Mount Sinai (and the two tablets of the Testimony were in Moses' hand when he came down from the mountain), that Moses did not know that the skin of his face shone while he talked with Him. So when

Aaron and all the children of Israel saw Moses, behold, the skin of his face shone, and they were afraid to come near him (Exodus 34:29-30).

After spending some time in the presence of God, Moses' face shone. Outwardly it was recognizable and could not remain hidden; everyone saw that Moses was changed. This word for *radiate*, used to describe Moses' face, is the Hebrew word *qaran* and can also mean "horn" or "horns," which is why Michelangelo placed horns on his famous statue of Moses, which can be seen in the San Pietro church at Vincoli in Rome. The sculpture, which is over two meters high, depicts Moses, and two horns protrude unmistakably from his head. Some attribute it to a translation error of the Vulgate, the Latin translation of the Bible, while others are convinced of its authenticity.

Whatever Moses looked like, one thing is clear—if we press through to the face of God, it will not go unnoticed. Our outer appearance will change, holiness and awe will shine from us, and even our fellow human beings will be moved by it. People will look at us and will be touched by what we carry within us. Then reactions will bubble up—some will be attracted, while others may react in a hostile way. As with Jesus—some let themselves be moved by Him and for others He was a stumbling block. Not everyone reacts to the glory as we would like them to.

MEN'S CONFERENCES

Three times in the year all your men shall appear before the Lord, the Lord God of Israel. For I will cast out the nations before you and enlarge your borders; neither will any man covet your land when you go up to appear before the Lord your God three times in the year (Exodus 34:23-24).

The glory of the face of God should really not be an option; rather, it is a must.

As Christians we pray for our country. We want to see God's plans come about. Laws as well as political, economic, and legal decisions should be implemented in our country in a godly way. None of this is merely wishful thinking—Jesus Himself left us the request in the Lord's Prayer: "Your kingdom come. Your will be done on earth as it is in heaven." It's not a fairy tale. I am firmly convinced that the world can reflect heaven. And we will do it successfully when we ascend to the glory of the face of God and from there fulfill God's charge to us on the earth, just as Moses spent time before the face of God for the only purpose of receiving instruction for an entire people and nation and for implementing this.

But that won't happen without men. We need men of the kingdom who seek God together. Heroes of faith whom children, women, and the world look up to—not passive couch potatoes but overcomers who take life and society into their hands; who are role models for children; who care for women and take responsibility in society; who hate injustice and fight for freedom for the oppressed; who do not see frustration as a cause for anger but for whom disappointments are the motivation to achieve breakthroughs; who are heroes who develop ambition in difficulties and do not give up.

166

In their communication they are clear, their faith is unshakable, their love lavish, they forgive instantly and are willing to fight at any time, they are exemplary in their work, have learned the fear of God, and are always seeking the face of God.

God commanded the Israelites to appear before God three times a year. They were to focus their eyes on what was holy, righteous, and precious. Their heart was not to be hardened but transformed. They needed regular times of rest—not rest from God, but from everyday life, from their activities. If they took that to heart, then God assured them success, security, peace, and His blessing for the whole people.

It is part of the destiny of men to come before the face of God, to deliberately make time for fellowship with the Most High. This is very important, and I cannot stress it enough; God has strongly connected the destiny of a nation with the calling of men. The blessing on a country lies in the hands of men of God, men of the kingdom. Let us pray for them, give them space, and support them.

Then the wonderful women of the kingdom will also be released for even greater effectiveness and fruit—these women to whom we owe so much today who, especially in the West, uphold Christianity, pray tirelessly, and often fill the vacuum we men have left through our passivity. When we as men stand up, we will make it easier for women to come before the face of God.

The glory of the face of God is not a choice but our duty if we want to see heaven invading earth.

*The glory of the face of God
is not a choice but our duty if we want
to see heaven invading earth.*

RELAY RACE

"Life isn't a sprint"—you might have heard that expression before. It's absolutely true. "It's a marathon," is often added. I don't entirely agree with that because both sprints and marathons are races that are decided exclusively by the individual runner. But life is not really like that. A relay race would be the more appropriate term—everyone has his own stretch to run, and yet everyone needs the others to win.

For heaven to come to earth, we are dependent on one another, but not only that—we are dependent on the believers who preceded us in the last decades and centuries and who paid an immensely high price for the kingdom. Previous generations had to fight their way through with much sweat and anguish and pay for achievements that we take so much for granted. We must never forget that.

And the future of our descendants also depends on how we run and how we hand over the baton to them. What legacy will we leave them? Will we hand over an egocentric Christianity, or are we role models they can emulate because we are continually moving toward the face of God? Are we enslaved to the zeitgeist, or do we, if necessary, swim against the current? Are we indifferent to the decay of society, or do we rise up when the profane is tolerated and the sacred desecrated? Do we show future generations how to criticize everything and everyone rather than spreading the kingdom of God in love, grace, and truth? What do we want to leave them?

What a testimony it would be if our generation were to go down in history as a generation that pressed in to the face of God and blessed humankind with a glory never seen before!

Let us look up to heaven together and see what it has to offer us. We want to keep praying, "On earth as it is in heaven!"

We can leave a legacy—one for which past and future generations will be eternally grateful. Let us rise up together, let us allow ourselves to be set on fire, and let us pay the price.

For us and our time it may seem unimaginable, but with God everything is possible. Therefore, we sigh together, "O Lord, we need You!"

LEVEL 9

UNITY WITH GOD

That they all may be one, as You, Father, are in Me, and I in You; that they also may be one in Us, that the world may believe that You sent Me. And the glory which You gave Me I have given them, that they may be one just as We are one: I in them, and You in Me; that they may be made perfect in one, and that the world may know that You have sent Me, and have loved them as You have loved Me (John 17:21-23).

I f you knew you were facing the worst time of your life, you would probably be sending your most evocative and perhaps most fervent prayers to Almighty God. Surprisingly, with Jesus it was prayer for unity. Just before the most dramatic twenty-four hours of His life, marked by horror, beatings, vilification, slander, hatred, torture, crucifixion, and finally death itself, Jesus found nothing more important than praying for unity.

Not only that, Jesus gives us the glory He had received from the Father for the sake of one thing only—that His body may be one. In other words, Jesus gives us glory, but in return He also expects unity.

171

I am excited at the idea of finding the body of Christ in unity. Think about how the world would be turned upside down in a short time and how much more like heaven the earth could be. How much more comfortable the Lord would feel among us.

I pray for unity, because Jesus Himself felt that this was the most important prayer request before His crucifixion—how could I not also be an advocate of this request myself!

Jesus Himself felt that this was the most important prayer request before His crucifixion.

At the same time, I am firmly convinced that this unity can only happen through the Spirit of God. It will not be man-made unity. It is not unity when Catholics and Protestants gather to sing the same songs. Nor is it unity when we limit ourselves to the lowest common denominator and push everything else aside.

Unity also does not mean that we gather around what we have in common and neglect the less important issues. Even if the differences are often marginal in relation to the similarities, we still need the intervention of the Holy Spirit, because in many ways the differences are important after all.

Unity will not happen if we simply omit the differences. And yet differences should not deter us from working for unity, seeking it, and even fighting for it in the face of all narrow-mindedness. This unity will come about through conviction from the Holy Spirit and not through invitations on our Facebook or Instagram pages.

And the Lord said, "Indeed the people are one and they all have one language, and this is what they begin to do; now nothing that they propose to do will be withheld from them" (Genesis 11:6).

UNITY CHANGES THE WORLD

Neither faith, nor prayer, nor grace can change the world, nor can love. Only unity will transform society. I hope I will not be misunderstood—to bring heaven to earth you need faith, prayer, grace, love, and much more. However, the decisive factor and the main ingredient for the reformation of the body of Christ and of the land and for transformation is unity. During the construction of the Tower of Babel, God acknowledged that the people had immense power to fulfill their own plans. Nothing would be impossible for them if they remained in this unity.

The devil and accuser of the saints is called the "god of this world," and for millennia he has been shaping the world through his own dominion. His army, his empire, and his agenda keep our world quite successfully in his clutches. How can Beelzebub maintain his success over such a long period?

The answer is unity. The kingdom of darkness does not exist through love—at any rate, I strongly doubt that there is even a spark of love between demons, powers, and principalities in the heavenlies. The realm of darkness endures because of its unity. All its subjects are concerned only with the mission assigned to them. They subordinate themselves to the greater good—in this case, of course, to the greater evil. They are aware of the fatal consequences for their empire if this unity were to be broken. This is precisely why they attack our unity—they know that the united body of Christ will bring down their kingdom.

Like-minded people who tackle something in unity and put aside their own vanity and egoism can change the world. No wonder Jesus prayed for unity.

But what does unity with God look like? Of course, Jesus is the perfect example. He subordinated every area of His life to the Father. On the one hand, He did not shy away from revealing His fears; but on the other, He did not allow himself to be controlled by them. Unity with His Father was His life's work; it permeated every physical and emotional area of His life and was the determining influence in His decisions, deeds, and works.

TWENTY-ONE SAINTS

I would claim that I have seen this level of glory before, in a propaganda video from the IS (Islamic State). This shows 21 Christians, on a beach in Libya being escorted to their execution by 21 slaughterers. Twenty-one men, 20 Coptic Christians and one brother from Ghana, who lost their earthly lives because of their faith in Jesus. (See Appendix.) This video, staged by radical Islamists, moved me deeply. No, it didn't shock me as its makers said it would; it moved me and strengthened my faith.

On February 15, 2015, a group defined by hatred and ignorance published this video. The scene took place on a beach near the Libyan port city of Sirte and was intended to spread fear and terror in the western world, the "world of the cross," as they call it. This ignorance alone shows their naïveté, to say the least. If they had only a little knowledge of the history of Christianity, they would know that martyrdom has never frightened followers of Jesus. Quite the opposite—Christianity was only made stronger by this and spread further.

In Europe and North and South America, this knowledge seems to have been lost, as if the persecution of Christians has been assigned to another epoch that has long since passed away. But nothing could be further from the truth. Almost daily, Christians in the Middle East, Far East, and Africa experience persecution, discrimination, humiliation, degradation, and martyrdom.

There was never an age in which Christians lived in complete safety and with total protection. Why do we no longer understand this form of Christianity, which in the West is viewed as a kind of relict of prehistoric times? Is it because faith has been downgraded to a private matter? Are we so far removed from the foundations on which Christianity is built, from the blood and death of many fellow believers and their steadfastness, even stubbornness, of faith?

In many old democratic cultures, we enjoy a more or less strict separation of church and state, which most people agree with, but we also see how faith is restricted. Living faith and missionary activity are demonized, while humanism is highly acclaimed, even if it tolerates abuses that are insufferable.

Of course, I do not wish for persecution in our country, which ends in murder, slaughter, and beheadings, but I honor the faith that does not wince at the dangers, smear campaigns, and "political correctness" that are common in western culture. I praise the faith that loves life, knowing that we serve a higher cause and that our true eternal reward is in heaven.

Back to the 21 brothers in the faith who were beheaded in Libya. The video clip, which was clicked and viewed hundreds of thousands of times, shows the merciless hatred that Christians are still exposed to in many parts of the world.

It is a dreary, cloudy day on a beach near Sirte; the sun cannot get through, the color of the sea is dark blue, the pleasing turquoise of the water is nowhere to be seen, and the few rays of sun do not penetrate into the depths of the water. In addition, the editors covered the entire film with a gray haze to intensify the desolate atmosphere.

The changing camera angles let us guess in how much detail the scenes were thought through and planned. Right after the first scene, the camera perspective changes to the right, away from the image of the waves of the sea toward the main protagonists of the message that is to be sent out to the world—21 men, most of them barefoot and dressed in orange overalls, plod slowly and with even steps through the damp grey sand that sinks under their feet and retains traces of their footprints.

Their hands tied behind them, they are accompanied by masked men who hold them by the collar or neck and assertively show them the way. The knives and daggers strapped around the upper body of the executioners, which in a few moments will be used as murder tools, are clearly visible.

Rocks protrude from the sand at irregular intervals and then the even pace of the men falters as they avoid them by taking a larger step. Subconsciously we hear the constant noise of the waves in the background.

With every step the men take toward us, their faces become clearer. They are Egyptians, migrant workers who left their families and loved ones behind to enable them to lead a better life or perhaps to finance education for their children. Among them a dark-skinned man stands out; later we learn that this is Matthew Ayariga from Ghana.

In the different camera angles, the faces can be quite clearly seen—and what surprises us is, no fear or terror can be seen on them. The facial features are not distorted or cramped; they are totally relaxed, perhaps even contented. Some people are moving their lips. They are praying or singing. These are the last steps of their earthly life and they dedicate them to their Lord Jesus.

Why this confidence in the faces of these heroes of the faith? Perhaps they had previously been tortured, beaten, and tormented; surely, they had been offered the chance of renouncing their faith for their lives to be spared. Were they struggling with fears, doubts, and inner conflict? We will only know in eternity.

The confidence and trust in their faces—do they perhaps come from the knowledge that they did not stumble in the face of terror and did not weaken in their faith? Is it the conviction that they will immediately receive their reward and victory wreath because they confessed Jesus and did not deny Him?

It is this steadfastness that for me defines this level of glory. One lives this life with gratitude and joy, but also in the awareness of finding something greater in the future age. The 11th chapter of the Epistle to the Hebrews contains a verse we find hard to understand nowadays.

Others were tortured, not accepting deliverance, that they might obtain a better resurrection (Hebrews 11:35).

It would be dishonest to say I understand this stance. But in union with God you see your own life through different eyes.

In union with God you see your own life through different eyes.

These 21 migrant workers were probably tortured and offered release, which they did not accept for the sake of Jesus and for a better resurrection.

They are lined up by side, their tormentors behind them, waiting for the end of the orchestrated scene. The men dressed in black push the shackled prisoners onto the ground in front of them one by one with their heads in the sand. They bend over them and lean with their knees on the backs of the 21 men dressed in orange.

They grasp their hair with their hands, pull their heads toward them, then they hold a knife to their throats. No one screams, no one begs for mercy, no one changes his mind, no one saves his life. Only gentle words are heard from the mouths of these peaceful faces. And then the last words before the deathblows, "*Jarap Jesoa!*" —Lord Jesus!

Then the camera pans again to the vastness of the sea, but now the water shimmers neither in turquoise nor dark blue, as we are used to from the beaches at the Mediterranean Sea. This water is red, soaked with the blood of these saints and martyrs.

Also I say to you, whoever confesses Me before men, him the Son of Man also will confess before the angels of God (Luke 12:8).

It breaks our hearts that such scenes still take place today, but it also fills us with joy to see such faith, confidence, and conviction that challenge and strengthen us.

They lost their lives to receive the eternal kingdom. At the end they were alone, bound by their tormentors, but in heaven they were received by hosts of angels, free forever. On earth they did not deny their faith, even in the face of death; in heaven Jesus confessed their names before the angels and before God. In their lives they were inconspicuous and unknown; in heaven everyone knows them, and they are heroes.

That is unity with God.

Martyrdom is not a prerequisite for experiencing this level of glory, and many will never have to experience it, thank God. But everyone will face difficulties and will come into situations where denying Jesus seems more sensible. To overcome such moments and to stand firmly in faith—these are the steps that lead us into this glory.

PATHS OF UNITY

And Enoch walked with God; and he was not, for God took him (Genesis 5:24).

Enoch is not a person we know from countless Bible stories. We do not have any great narratives about him or stories full of miracles. And yet he is one of the most fascinating characters in the Word of God. Only two passages in the Bible give us a glimpse of Enoch's life, but these are all the more extraordinary.

In Hebrews 11:5, Enoch's extraordinary faith is praised, although nothing unusual is attributed to it other than that by faith he ascended to exhilarating spiritual heights and was raptured. He did not see death and was raptured by God because he received a testimony of good pleasure. God looked at Enoch and was so pleased with what He saw—without further ado, He took Enoch and placed him in eternity to enjoy unity with God.

How did this happen? His faith was evident in his walk with God. The Bible says, "He walked with God!" He was so strongly moved by God and so incredibly devoted to Him that he was one with God.

Unity with God is also the glory in which Adam and Eve lived before the Fall. Wherever God went, they also went, and what they saw God doing, they also imitated. It was perfect unity and glory—unity with God.

Their decision against the counsel of God removed them from this glorious realm and suddenly God had to call out for them.

And they heard the sound of the Lord God walking in the garden in the cool of the day, and Adam and his wife hid themselves from the presence of the Lord God among the trees of the garden. Then the Lord God called to Adam and said to him, "Where are you?" (Genesis 3:8-9)

They were no longer one with God. Remoteness had developed between them and their Creator. The voice of God was no longer close; they now heard it as if far away. They were no longer solely devoted to the Almighty but took time out from God to pursue their debased lusts. When God spoke, He could no longer rely on being heard or perceived by man. Outside of this level of glory, God must "search" for us, demand our attention, and convict us again and again so that we approach Him.

For all have sinned and fall short of the glory of God (Romans 3:23).

Sin and glory are two forces that cannot coexist. They are two opposites that cannot be brought together. They are inhomogeneous, and there is an immovable dividing line between them.

Draw near to God and He will draw near to you (James 4:8).

This level of God's presence can no longer be taken for granted. It requires our commitment, willingness, and obedience to approach God with sanctification, purification, and self-sacrifice. Because that's what pleases God. It delights Him so much that He doesn't just wait until we come to Him. No, He personally shortens the path and the distance between us by coming to meet us at the same time.

It's a glorious presence, but it is costly.

GLORIOUS BUT COSTLY

Though He was a Son, yet He learned obedience by the things which He suffered (Hebrews 5:8).

Devotion is one of the prerequisites for this glory, and even Jesus had to learn the obedience that leads to this level of glory in difficult times and circumstances.

When I intercede, I pray to the Lord that He will fill us with faith, understanding, peace, devotion, and joy as we encounter many temptations and persecutions, knowing that we are on our way to the next glory.

Beloved, do not think it strange concerning the fiery trial which is to try you, as though some strange thing happened to you; but rejoice to the extent that you partake of Christ's sufferings, that when His glory is revealed, you may also be glad with exceeding joy. If you are reproached for the name of Christ, blessed are you, for the Spirit of glory and of God rests upon you. On their part He is blasphemed, but on your part He is glorified (1 Peter 4:12-14).

I would love to be more encouraging and wish I could tell you how wonderful and easy it is to get into this glory, but then I would be a deceiver. This level of glory is only for those who are willing to pay an immense price for it. God often assigns His glory to the unpleasant things of life.

This level of glory is only for those who are willing to pay an immense price for it.

Glory in Injustice (Proverbs 20:3)

To endure situations that are totally unjust—when we would most like to hit out with a hammer, but then don't do it—this is what God uses in order to personally intervene for us. Sometimes it takes time for us to see the meaning in it. But do not shut yourself off from the glory of God; give up your pride. Take Jesus as your model—He suffered injustice innocently and was rewarded with great glory.

Glory in Accusation (Exodus 14:10)

People will misunderstand you, misjudge your motives, and totally misunderstand your love. Do not allow the devil to involve you in disputes and discussions but forgive and trust the Lord and you will see His glory appear.

Glory in Persecution and Reproach for the Name of Christ (1 Peter 4:14)

To consider ourselves fortunate in persecution does not really seem to correspond to our nature, but that is exactly what Peter tells us. More than an injustice, even if it definitely is that, it is an honor to be persecuted and reviled for the sake of Jesus.

I remember a situation in India when we prayed for five or six pastors who had been unjustly arrested and imprisoned. They were experiencing some difficult days in prison, and we were praying for their release. Miraculously, all the charges against them were ultimately dropped and they were able to return home. We were overjoyed at this good news and praised God for His faithfulness.

When we welcomed the pastors with waving flags, their attitude impressed us the most. Instead of being tired, broken, angry, and bitter, they rejoiced because they were judged worthy to be persecuted and reviled for the name of Jesus. What an attitude—one that will be rewarded with eternal glory!

Glory in Dishonor (1 Corinthians 15:43)

Our carnal character tends to egoism and seeks honor. Galatians 5:20 mentions enmities, strife, jealousy, outbursts of rage, selfishness, quarrels, factions, and envy as qualities that correspond to this.

But glory is assigned to us for the opposite of these. When we are publicly honored and celebrated, it feels so good, but it is not often very beneficial. Rather, God rewards the things that tend to be inconspicuous or despised. Deeds and works that do not receive public attention and are even disregarded, so-called things of dishonor, do not remain unnoticed by God.

Perhaps your part in the kingdom of God feels unimportant and meaningless because it does not receive much attention; however, do not be deceived, but remind yourself that God has prepared eternal glory for your ministry.

Glory Through Humility (Proverbs 15:33)

Humility precedes glory. Humility does not always feel good, and sometimes we would like to have a break from it, but from glory to glory it becomes more and more rooted in our personality and God rewards that with even more glory. When the Lord sees humility, it moves Him to generosity, and He rewards us boundlessly.

When the Lord sees humility,
it moves Him to generosity,
and He rewards us boundlessly.

Glory in Giving (Psalm 112:9)

Giving is more blessed than receiving (see Acts 20:31). When we are provided for or given presents, it feels so great and we sense the love that is being shown to us. Provision is the way God deals with His children. But to provide for others and to give without expecting anything will be rewarded with glory. Jesus even said that if we have nothing to give, then we should sell something to bless the needy (see Luke 12:33). By this Jesus means that our own lack should not prevent us from giving, for this opens up the glory of God to us.

Glory of Intimacy (James 4:8)

This requires us to make time to spend with God. When we approach Him, He runs toward us and gives us the gift of His presence and glory. This does not mean that we should neglect our responsibilities in the family, work, and the church; it is merely about our priorities—God and His righteousness first, and He'll take care of everything else.

What is the price we pay for glory realms like "unity with God"? It is living in humility, being generous in spite of need, seeking God, suffering injustice, finding joy in persecution, enduring accusations, and doing things for which others feel they are too good or too spiritual.

But I can encourage us with the many stories of the heroes of the faith who have gone before us, who overcame the difficulties and received their reward—our forerunners, who paid an enormous price and sometimes did not know how they would survive the next day. These experiences were not easy and yet each of these followers of Jesus would tell us how worthwhile it was and that they would do it again for the prize and reward they received afterward.

I can encourage us because God strengthens us on this path, allowing us to experience miracles and His extraordinary power. We may see God and feel His heartbeat and the breath of His mouth. On this path there is joy and contentment, stillness and peace, balance and fulfilment, confidence and faith, strength and trust, gratitude and courage, all of which we do not experience on any other path, no matter what our circumstances are.

Come near to God, pursue Him, rejoice and be glad, and then the Lord will come near to you! What greater reward could we have?

THE UNAPPROACHABLE LIGHT

In historic times and in the ancient world, countless people experienced God, they knew Him, and many of them were privileged to see God. Some even walked with Him and others enjoyed unity with God. This was not only in the past. There are still people today who are willing to pay the price to advance to these levels of glory.

And then there is this one level of the glory of God, which caused John to make the following statement:

No one has seen God at any time (1 John 4:12).

Think about it for a minute; he says *no one* has ever seen God. Neither Moses or Abraham, Isaiah or John, nor even Adam and Eve—there is no man who was ever allowed or able to see God at this highest level of glory! This place or realm is reserved exclusively for God, and that will not change for all eternity. He is God and therefore He alone is worthy to occupy a place that corresponds utterly to His divinity and His being. No one else will ever be granted this privilege, for there is no one who is good but God (see Mark 10:18). The Lord our God, the Lord is one (see Deut. 6:4)!

This exclusive place and realm of glory is called "the unapproachable light."

> *Which He will manifest in His own time, He who is the blessed and only Potentate, the King of kings and Lord of lords, who alone has immortality, dwelling in unapproachable light, whom no man has seen or can see, to whom be honor and everlasting power. Amen* (1 Timothy 6:15-16).

There are many rulers or lords in the world, but only one Lord of lords. Countless kings have lived in the past millennia and yet there is only one King of kings. He is not only immortal, He possesses immortality; He is so far above everything that He assigns immortality. God alone inhabits unapproachable light, and no one has ever seen Him in this, because there is no one who even remotely compares to God's wonderful being. The Almighty decided to live in us (see Col. 1:27) and we can be in Him (see 2 Cor. 5:17), but in the end God is always God and man is always man!

God alone inhabits unapproachable light,
and no one has ever seen Him in this,
because there is no one who even remotely
compares to God's wonderful being.

I love Isaiah 44:6-8, for it resounds like the judge's gavel when He announces the final judgment, leaving no room for doubt about truth and fact.

Thus says the Lord, the King of Israel, and his Redeemer, the Lord of hosts: "I am the First and I am the Last; besides Me there is no God. And who can proclaim as I do? Then let him declare it and set it in order for Me, since I appointed the ancient people. And the things that are coming and shall come, let them show these to them. Do not fear, nor be afraid; have I not told you from that time, and declared it? You are My witnesses. Is there a God besides Me? Indeed there is no other Rock; I know not one" (Isaiah 44:6-8).

It is clear that God is worthy to inhabit a place that is not accessible to anyone else. He is the first and the last; He incorporates everything. There is no one who is worthy even to raise his voice and to dispute God's position. God who knows everything—there is no one known to Him who could even come close to Him. There is no one else who is like God!

JESUS IS GOD

In the preceding chapters we saw levels of glory to which God invites us and which He shares with us (see John 17:22), which are also necessary for the fulfillment of destinies. Nevertheless, there is an exclusiveness about the unapproachable light; it is reserved for God and is neither for men nor for angels; only God, the Father, the Son, and the Holy Spirit, and no one else dwells here. He does not share it with anyone else—never and without exception.

And I will not give My glory to another (Isaiah 48:11).

Apart from Jesus, no one has ever seen God, because Jesus Himself is God.

No one has seen God at any time. The only begotten Son, who is in the bosom of the Father, He has declared Him (John 1:18).

Jesus can make the Father known because He is one with Him and enjoys His abode even in the highest regions of the glory of God. He had been like God (see Phil. 2:6), but humbled Himself for the redemption of the world, whereupon He became like us (see Phil. 2:7). God's Son gave up His life on the cross, not to lose it, but to win the world. Finally, the Father raised Him again to the highest heights of glory, to the unapproachable light from which He had descended before, far above every name and every created thing, whether earthly or heavenly (see Phil. 2:9-10).

Jesus blessed all those who believe—far more than we could ever deserve. He forgives us our sins, redeems us, gives us eternal life, gives us the authority of His name, shares His glory with us, blesses us with healing, opens heaven to us, lets us do the same works and even greater ones, and we enjoy His glory even though He alone is responsible for everything. Together with Him we may even sit on His throne and will ourselves judge angels.

As wonderful as that is, it can even go to our heads. In the end, all this is His merit and His alone, so there is also a place that can only be inhabited by Him.

Enoch was raptured because God took Him to Himself (see Gen. 5:24). Even Elijah went up to heaven in the storm, accompanied by the fiery chariots of God (see 2 Kings 2:11). John received an invitation to heaven and was transferred there to receive revelations for the body of Christ (see Rev. 4:1).

But no one ever ascended the highest level of glory except Jesus, who alone is glorious enough because He once descended from this realm Himself. Enoch, Elijah, and John ascended to heaven, but Jesus sat down at the farthest sides of the north. That is why, in spite of Enoch, Elijah, and John, John 3:13 correctly and unmistakably tells us that no one has ascended into heaven except Jesus Himself!

No one has ascended to heaven but He who came down from heaven, that is, the Son of Man who is in heaven (John 3:13).

NO ONE IS LIKE GOD

And the heavens will praise Your wonders, O Lord; Your faithfulness also in the assembly of the saints. For who in the heavens can be compared to the Lord? Who among the sons of the mighty can be likened to the Lord? God is greatly to be feared in the assembly of the saints, and to be held in reverence by all those around Him. O Lord God of hosts, who is mighty like You, O Lord? Your faithfulness also surrounds You. You rule the raging of the sea; when its waves rise, You still them. You have broken Rahab in pieces, as one who is slain; You have scattered

Your enemies with Your mighty arm. The heavens are Yours, the earth also is Yours; the world and all its fullness, You have founded them (Psalm 89:5-11).

No one is like God. Indeed, no one is even approximately comparable to Him. His are the heavens and the earth; therefore, there is nothing that would not be subject to His authority and power. God is God, and there is no other!

Now to the King eternal, immortal, invisible, to God who alone is wise, be honor and glory forever and ever. Amen (1 Timothy 1:17).

He is King, He has always been King, and will always be King. He alone is worthy of all honor, worship, and glory; He is immortal, invisible, and God alone.

He is our God. Our King. Our Father. Our Savior. He is wonderful and magnificent. Amen!

PATHS TO GREATER GLORY

———◆———

Perhaps you have already read some books about glory and are a seeker of the greater glory of God. Perhaps you have already experienced glory in one of the forms mentioned and would like to take with you all that glory still has to offer. It may be that you associate glory only with the overlapping of heaven and earth or limit it exclusively to signs and wonders and that new aspects have been opened up to you through this book.

It is impossible to deal adequately with the boundlessness of the glory of God in a book like this. There are certainly still some areas that are unrecognized or barely known. That is why I pray, as I did at the beginning, that the Holy Spirit will use the words of this book and open up depths of glory to us that go far beyond what we have covered here.

God's desire is to share His glory with us. We are called to be partakers of His glory (see 1 Pet. 5:1). There is nothing that He wants to withhold from us; in Christ He has given us everything else as well.

For it was fitting for Him, for whom are all things and by whom are all things, in bringing many sons to glory, to make the captain of their salvation perfect through sufferings (Hebrews 2:10).

Greater glory is not just an alternative to our present life; it is God's desire and the reason Jesus endured suffering and crucifixion. Yes, salvation and our sanctification are the main reason for the path Christ took, but they are not the only motive.

The redeemed, the saved, the justified, and the children of God have already received their salvation, so what about them? Are they just destined to wait until they can finally go to heaven? Should they merely drag themselves through life and its challenges in the coming years and decades?

Nothing seems to be further from the truth and yet, unfortunately, for many it feels that way. Their only hope seems to be that at the end they will at least reach the finish line of their personal race, panting and powerless. Emaciated and worn out, they dare to believe that God in heaven still has a crown of victory for them. We can be sure that He has much more for us.

But not only in heaven. We can already experience heavenly glory here and live in it. There are many sons whom He led and is leading to glory. Not all, but many. Not because He arbitrarily rejects some, but because many decide against it. However, we are all called to obtain the glory of Christ (see 2 Thess. 2:14).

In God's boundless grace and justice, He lets us participate in His glory. Personally, God healed me from physical suffering before

I ever did anything for Him. I experienced signs and miracles before I was even remotely worthy. He redeemed me, healed me, sanctified me, justified me, embraced me, kissed me, saved me, and guided me although I did not know Him, let alone focus my life on His ways.

In God's boundless grace and justice,
He lets us participate in His glory.

How wonderful and merciful this God is. He is not only my God; He has also given me the right to call Him Father and Daddy. I could never have even begun to earn what God simply gave me.

Today He is still so incredibly generous. He does far more than we can think of or ask for. He hears our prayers and grants us our desires, not according to the excellence of our words, but according to His own strength.

In Second Thessalonians 2:14 it says we are to obtain the glory of Christ. This word *obtain* is the Greek word *peripoiesis* and means "buy" or "acquire." Not that we can acquire it as mortal beings, as we could not possibly pay that price. God wants to see our willingness: What price are we willing to pay? For the way to the greatest levels of glory seems to be paved with difficulties, with rejection, insult, slander, misunderstanding, abuse, persecution, and other trouble.

For I consider that the sufferings of this present time are not worthy to be compared with the glory which shall be revealed in us (Romans 8:18).

Following these paths for the glory of God is well worthwhile. Let us pray together for a desire and a passion that will make us take this path with joy. We want to be so radically in love with Jesus that all the sufferings of the present time are of no consequence in the face of the anticipation and reward of future glory.

Perhaps we unconsciously think that we need to be perfect and complete for these levels of glory. But that is absolutely not true. God calls us imperfect beings to this glory; He is the one who leads us to perfection, not our own efforts. Our Father in heaven only wants to see that we do not deride His holiness and glory.

Even saints are only simple sinners who refuse to make peace with sin. Our prayers are imperfect too—how could it be otherwise? Therefore, God does not answer them according to how perfect they are but according to His own power, grace, love, and mercy.

Richard Hooker, an English theologian from the 16th century, describes this in his sermon on justification as follows: "Even our best and most exquisite works have something in them that must be sanctified, cleansed and forgiven."[1]

J.C. Ryle, the first Anglican bishop of Liverpool, said: "Even in our best works there is imperfection. We do not love God to the